W9-BEU-375

Sports Medicine, Notre Dame

Sports Medicine, Notre Dame

The Life and Times
of a Sports Medicine Specialist
at the University of Notre Dame

by
Leslie M. Bodnar, MD

Sports Medicine, Notre Dame
Copyright © 2014 Leslie M. Bodnar, MD

All rights reserved. No part of this book may be used or reproduced in any manner whatsoever without the written permission of the publisher.

10 9 8 7 6 5 4 3 2

ISBN 978-0-9912451-4-7

Corby Books
P.O. Box 93
Notre Dame, Indiana 46556
www.corbypublishing.com

Printed in the United States of America

*This work is dedicated
to my understanding wife and family,
without whose love and support
nothing would have been possible*

Randy Harrison's recent response to questions about the injury: "Here is what I remember. The picture was taken after I broke my arm on the last play of the first half against Purdue my junior year, in 1976. The Purdue quarterback (Gary Danielson, I believe) threw a "Hail Mary Pass" down the sideline (we had a big lead). I went up for the ball and, as I swatted it away, I made hard contact with the receiver. When we both came down, I felt my arm snap and then the pain! I realized my arm was injured. Both bones in my forearm were broken. I had surgery for that. It required plates and screws to stabilize the bones. I didn't recover in time to play in the Gator Bowl that year, but I came back the following year as good as new! There was a silver lining to this unfortunate situation. That injury resulted in me being granted another year of eligibility, so I was then able to become the first winner of five football monograms."

Contents

Foreword

by Ara Parseghian

DR. LES BODNAR has written this book filled with memories of his thirty-five years in Sports Medicine at the University of Notre Dame and the unique experience of working with seven different head football coaches. He relates his thoughts and experiences with each and explores the many changes in the care of these athletes and in the orthopaedic procedures performed during his tenure.

If you are a sports fan, you have seen the contest interrupted due to an injury many times. You have seen the doctor and trainers run out on the field to attend to the downed player. In most cases, the athlete recovers and continues participation. What happens when the patient is carted off the field?

This book will give you an insight and perspective of what a doctor is confronted with. In his case, Dr. Bodnar, the Notre Dame orthopaedic surgeon, will take you through the medical demands of the job and the necessity of building relationships with coaches and many others to establish credibility. School officials, parents, and players must all be supportive. He will tell you how difficult it is to deny a player participation because of a physical disqualification. He will tell you of his relationship with the seven football head coaches he worked with during his tenure. This included yours

Ara Parseghian, the determined and highly successful Head Football Coach at the University of Notre Dame (1964-1974).

truly. He is a bit too complimentary with his kind words, but it is very nice to hear after so many years have passed.

Dr. Bodnar will take you through many of the key games that Notre Dame played during his career: undefeated seasons, National Championships, Bowl Games and other important contests. He will describe a few key games in which the medical team contributed to the successful outcome of the contest. This book is obviously slanted toward Notre Dame Football, but any sports fan will enjoy reading the doctor's view of what sports medicine is all about. He was on top of all the action, so you are hearing it firsthand.

Football coaches are under great pressure to win. Just think about a doctor in charge of the health of an entire team. The outcome of a game is one thing—having the lives of all the participants in your hands is huge. Dr. Bodnar successfully managed thirty-five years of such responsibility. It was beneficial to us. His work was appreciated.

Coach Ara Parseghian

Introduction
~ A Brief History of Sports Medicine ~

IN ABOUT 1949, sports medicine was evolving as a special area in the practice of orthopaedic surgery. This had come about gradually, as a response to the ever-increasing concentration on sports in today's world. Certain conditions commonly treated by the orthopaedic surgeon were found to be especially frequent in sports. These included knee injuries, shoulder dislocations, muscle and tendon problems—such as those due to overuse as is "tennis elbow"—and others. Some sports presented a particular predilection for one or another condition, such as the severe knee injuries in football.

Many other disciplines were interested and involved in various aspects of the care of the athlete, whether it be the care of his feet, his eyes, his brain or other parts. This also stimulated research into the total cerebro-musculoskeletal functioning of the athlete. As a result, multiple organizations entered the field. The orthopaedic surgeon came to be recognized as the expert in most of the more serious musculoskeletal injuries in sports. Those physicians associated with athletic teams and athletes had specific interests and goals in the care of their athletes. It was their job to understand the nature and demands of the sport in which the athlete participated and to return him to competition safely and promptly. It required that the doctor be familiar with whatever measures applied—such as taping, bracing, rehabilitation methods and others—in addition to whatever medical knowledge would best serve their athlete and the team. Injuries outside the musculoskeletal system were referred to the care of other specialists in their fields: neurosurgeons, ENT specialists, cardiologists, dentists, etc.

The orthopaedist had a major role in the care of these men at the college level. Their care was relegated to the medical staff of the University. At high school and lower levels, it was the internist, pediatrician, and/or family doctor who played the most important role. These men were the primary source in the general care of the developing athlete, conducting routine pre-season examinations and lending their presence to athletic events in their communities. They were the unsung heroes in so many cases, giving of their time and services as volunteers.

With the popularity of sports, the term "sports medicine" came to be applied to a wide variety of enterprises capitalizing on the term. Sports medicine came to be a "buzz" word for that glamorous branch of medicine and related sciences concerned with athletic performance. This required knowledge of not only the treatment of conditions incurred in sports, but also all that goes before and after—the physiology, kinesiology, weight training, protective equipment, safety measures, splinting and first aid; the diagnosis, treatment, and rehabilitation of injuries; and the research associated with the above—in order to best serve the athlete and his team and to facilitate the prized athlete's prompt return to his sport.

In that era during which I served as orthopaedic consultant and team doctor at Notre Dame, from 1949 to 1985, there were many changes in the treatment of athletic injuries. Some of the major developments during my time included early surgery for ligament injuries of the knee, and the development of arthroscopic surgery allowing diagnosis and treatment with minimal invasion of the body and with less pain, blood loss, and time of recovery. In addition, new protective equipment was designed and new rules were established to protect the player. The relationships were also changing between the physicians, the patient-athletes, the athletic coaches, and the trainers.

I write to record my experiences and my observations during my years with the University of Notre Dame and of the changes in sports-medicine during that period. This discussion also requires at least a profile view of the administration and principal persons with whom I worked during that time.

Notre Dame
1949

In 1949, Notre Dame was a small, all-male, Midwest, Catholic university of about three-thousand students, including graduate students. It had an overarching reputation in the world of football, which was in contrast to its size—especially in comparison with the size of the major universities with which it competed in sports. Its reputation in football in those earlier years far exceeded its academic reputation. To some it was known as a "Football Factory," much to the chagrin of some among the Notre Dame Hierarchy at the time.

In a small school such as this, there was a close feeling between the students and the athletes. These athletes were the personal heroes of the student body and the alumni, including the "subway alumni," those followers of Notre Dame who had never attended the school but considered it their team. This included all those across the country with Irish blood in their veins. The Notre Dame team had once been known as "The Ramblers"; they were now known as the "Fighting Irish." And it was not only the Irish who wanted sainthood bestowed on the Notre Dame coaches and players; it was the legions of the poor and the downtrodden of every nationality, looking for a standard bearer on whom they could pin their hopes with a better chance for success than they usually met in their daily lives. They were the subway alumni and the Notre Dame football team was their team.

During my early years there, Notre Dame's success was made possible by virtue of the numbers and quality of the young men desiring to play ball there and the capable coaching to which they were subjected. Many good players were attracted to the school because of its reputation, and many good Catholic boys were steered toward the school by their families and by their high school mentors. In addition, World War II was over and, as the troops returned to civilian life, many decided to return to school. This was made easier by the G.I. Bill, by which the government gave financial support to those who would take advantage of it on leaving the Armed Services. This included those who had football in mind as well as academics, some of whom had already been playing on the virtually semi-pro football teams in the Armed Services.

These ex-servicemen swelled the ranks of the potentially fine athletes engaged in college sports in that day. These men were welcomed heartily by the college coaches: strong young men, well-developed and goal-oriented men who understood the discipline necessary to achieve their goals. Notre Dame had its share of these men. It was from this group of players, many of them no longer boys, among whom Notre Dame found the talent to compete once more for the National Championships in football.

A Beginning
in Sports Medicine

NOTRE DAME WAS DECLARED National Champions in college football on numerous occasions over the years. In 1949, the team was once again destined to have a championship football team under Coach Frank Leahy, who was the Head Coach when I first became involved in sports medicine at the University. It came as somewhat of a surprise when the opportunity to work at Notre Dame presented itself, one that changed my goals, my career, and my life. It gained recognition for me as one of the early orthopaedic surgeons concentrating on sports trauma.

At that time, I had been in South Bend, Indiana, for almost two years, seeking to establish my private practice of orthopaedic surgery. It was the custom at that time to establish an individual practice. I was still waiting for those opportunities when my training and experience would be put to good use in my slowly developing practice. I had time on my hands. I eyed the Notre Dame Program hopefully.

My invitation to participate in the program came as the result of an accident. In 1948, the physician responsible for medical care at Notre Dame was in an automobile accident. As a result, he was unable to continue with his work there. He was replaced by Dr. Sherman Egan—a capable Mayo-trained internist, who was appointed to the position of Director of Medical Care for the University. This involved the care of the students and student-athletes, as well as the large body of religious associated with the school.

Doctor Egan was very capable in his own field, but he did not feel comfortable looking after the traumatic conditions incurred by the student body in sports and in other ways. He realized that he would soon find himself in unfamiliar waters and decided that he would need help when it came to caring for the injuries suffered by the spirited and athletic all-male student body and the athletes at Notre Dame.

Dr. Robert Denham, a well-qualified orthopaedic surgeon, had arrived in the South Bend community just before I did. Dr. Egan offered him the opportunity to serve as orthopaedic consultant to the University. Dr. Denham accepted Dr. Egan's offer to work with the students and athletes and he performed the work capably. However, I'm not sure he really enjoyed the work. He was a quiet, dignified fellow, only slightly older than I, and also just out of the Armed Services. He was an excellent orthopaedist and a fine gentleman accustomed to making cautious and responsible decisions that he expected would be followed without question or controversy.

By the next year, Dr. Denham decided that the job did not suit him well, and he asked me to share the program. He offered the fall program to me. I don't know if it was because of his preference for bird-hunting in the fall, or the questioning of his medical decisions by the coaches and athletes in the fall of the previous year which caused him to give me what would have been my first choice, if the choice were mine. I, and the associates who were to join me as time went on, were to cover the fall semester, while Dr. Denham and his associates, Drs. Al Dingley and Earl Heller, assumed the work in the spring. This arrangement, sharing the work between our two offices on a semesterly basis, went on for many years, later becoming unified under my care. I accepted the appointment as orthopaedic consultant to the University in 1949. I was to have a close association with the athletic teams and the athletes at Notre Dame, the student body, and the clergy. I was entering foreign territory. I was not an athlete. This was a new world to me. I had gone directly into the Army from my orthopaedic residency at Charity Hospital in New Orleans, and as a result, up to this time, I had treated many more civilian and war casualties than athletes. However, I did bring to the job my training in the principles in the management of trauma, which applied equally to athletes, members of the armed services, and the general public. It seemed not to matter that I was not an athlete; more important to the job was my education, the years of training as a resident, and my experience in the Army as an orthopaedic surgeon, all of which prepared me to deal with trauma, including that of sports. I was qualified for the position in that way. The experience of dealing with coaches, athletes, and trainers was yet to come.

My assignment meant two clinics each week at the student infirmary to take care of the injured referred by the University physicians and a Sunday morning clinic in the trainers' room for injuries to the athletes. I was available at all times for emergencies and even for some routine consultations to return a player to action. These frequent demands led to daily visits to the athletic center at the end of my workday to avoid disruptions in my practice routines.

Facilities were available in the student infirmary for those who required observation or assisted care. Injured players might require such care if encumbered with large casts on one or another extremity, but as a rule these fellows would manage well after a few days with the assistance of their fellow students.

On occasions, a player injured at an away game might require hospitalization overnight for a head injury or some other condition. More often the injured were brought back to campus if their condition allowed, where they were hospitalized in the student infirmary or admitted to St. Joseph Hospital if need be. Then, back to classes as soon as reasonable. If necessary, they were supplied with golf carts to get them to class and to their dormitories.

It was not unusual on game day to see an athlete appearing happy and carefree in a golf cart, leg in a long leg cast propped-up on the cowl, with several other students and girls riding comfortably with him to the game. They are an adaptable lot.

The girls in the cart are an adaptation to a change in the environment at the campus of Our Lady. Notre Dame went co-ed in 1972. Women at St. Mary's College across the road had been allowed to take courses at Notre Dame as early as 1965. Women were initially resented by the all-male student body. The school had been rather proud of its all-male heritage. However, with the aforementioned adaptability of the students, this resentment did not last long, as witnessed by the girls in the cart.

The male students now accepted the presence of women on campus. And they did not treat them as they would their sister or their mother. They agreed that the good fathers had made a move in the right direction.

With this change, came other adjustments. The women flocked to athletics as did the men. Under government fiat, Title IX required that facilities for sports and other arrangements be available to women, just as for men. Compliance was a problem at first, but was soon functioning well. Locker rooms, a trainer's room, and other facilities were provided for the women's sports programs and teams. The University also contracted with female coaches and a female trainer to attend to their needs. One of our group was assigned to treat their orthopaedic concerns. The number of women's sports and the number of participants were few at first. During my time, no serious or unusual problems occurred

Women's basketball has developed into one of the prime sports venues at Notre Dame with the stimulus of Title IX, which requires opportunities and facilities for sports for women equal to those of men. Within the last few years this has led to excellence in the women's basketball program, leading to opportunities in the field of women's professional basketball as in the case of Skylar Diggins, class of 2013 seen here, and Kyla McBride, and Natalie Ochonwa, class of 2014.

among the female athletes during the first few years when I was assigned to their care in addition to my usual responsibilities. One of their more frequent problems was that of partial dislocations of the kneecap. Treatment was usually quite simple. A knitted or neoprene sleeve with an opening into which the patella fit allowed the kneecap to move more securely. Surgical measures were rarely employed for this. Over the years, the numbers of these young ladies playing on the women's sports teams increased. These athletes also required medical care. They received the care and facilities dictated by Title IX.

The Early Years

IN GENERAL, MY ASSOCIATION with the Notre Dame teams was a stimulating and, at times, an exciting job. Although a time-consuming job, it was also the bright spot in my daily activities, but it was not always a bed of roses.

It was a strain at times: the demands on my time, the travel, the long hours, the special arrangements to be made for the care of my patients in my absence, and those troublesome occasions when disaster struck—a serious injury. At such times, if surgery were indicated it would be necessary to explain the nature of the injury and the proposed treatment to the athlete, his family, and the coach. It took time and some pains to assure everyone that the condition had been carefully evaluated, that the decision was a well-considered one, and that the advised treatment was necessary. Those were often teary-eyed sessions. I have seen these young men tighten up to hold back their emotions.

I've also seen them turn away to hide their tears, like youngsters that some of them really are, some only eighteen and nineteen years of age. I've seen the moistened eyes of the parents as they tried to comfort the youth, even coaches, holding back their disappointment and grief. Lots of lip biting to control emotions, to "be a man" about it—not easy for the young athlete who can see the end of his playing that year, maybe even permanently. He is aware too that all his hard work to earn a position on the team has suddenly come to naught, that he may or may not win his position back, and he knows it will certainly not be handed back to him. He will have to earn it all over again—not an easy job.

It is at this stage that coaches and others may wish to alter the decisions. Maybe they can get another doctor to advise otherwise. Are we sure? How do we know? Can't we just try it and see? Maybe we can get him through the season? All the possibilities run through everyone's heads. Players went off for second opinions. They often found that the consultant not only agreed with the recommended action, but further suggested that our experience was most likely greater than theirs with such problems, and back they came.

During my career at Notre Dame, I worked with seven different coaches. As in most real-life situations, it is necessary to establish good working relationships with your co-workers, and this applied equally to working with the coaches of the athletic teams. The coaches all differed in their attitudes and expectations, methods and protocols, and in their compliance and understanding. It also behooved the physician to adapt to the conditions which thereby resulted. My indoctrination into this world was in the era of Coach Frank Leahy. I had much to learn in working under him. Those first few years taught me what to expect and what went on in that world.

In the earlier days of my time on the job, coaches were undergoing a transition in their thinking on this subject. In some cases, they had to be weaned from their earlier experiences in which they could get these opinions changed to suit their needs, manipulating doctors and trainers, as well as the all-too-willing athlete, even when not to the long-term advantage of the player. Coaches did gradually learn that with proper diagnosis and treatment more players could be salvaged for the team. Surgery was no longer viewed as an end-point in an athlete's career.

It took time to make it understood by all that these were medical not coaching decisions. This became firmly understood after Father Joyce established the policy regarding medical decisions—that the word of the doctor would be followed in medical matters.

The place of the orthopaedic surgeon as one of the members of the medical team working with the athletic teams was gaining acceptance. It took time and patience to establish this. And that was how it was when I entered the field of sports medicine, which only then was about to be recognized as an area of special expertise.

I learned in time the problems that might face the doctor who regarded the athlete as a patient, ahead of the aspirations of the coaches and ahead of the athlete's desire to return to play, when it was clearly not a safe and reasonable action. I was eager to cooperate but not to the extent that I was willing to compromise the athlete's welfare. Most coaches showed due concern for their athletes and required detailed explanation at times, but they were usually reasonable men. It was important to return the athlete to play as soon as possible, and that required fine-tuned judgment at times on the field and on the sidelines as well as at other less stressful moments.

It was especially difficult at those times when the athlete might be feeling well himself, convinced that he was a "fast healer," fully rehabilitated and that he was ready to go "full blast," or that he should be allowed to play because he could tolerate the pain of his condition. It was difficult at such times to convince the player that returning to play before the condition or injury was fully healed and rehabilitated would likely lead to recurrence of the condition—if we tried to take shortcuts. A fracture could have healed but the bony union had not yet strengthened to the degree compatible with the rigors of daily life on the field of sports. Premature return could lead to disaster.

There were exceptions. Some conditions, such as bruises and sprains, could be almost fully healed and a player could return to action without endangering himself. Even here, a fine point in decision-making was involved. If the condition was still painful, premature return to play could be detrimental to the team.

Such was the case with Nick Eddy in the 1966 game with Michigan State. There was some residual tenderness of the acromio-clavicular joint, which he had injured a few weeks earlier. As he was getting off the train the day of the Michigan State game in 1966, he slipped and jammed the shoulder causing recurrence of the pain. Injection of a local anesthetic into the injured acromio-clavicular joint of the shoulder did not relieve the sensitivity of the joint. A hard blow to it, which occurs frequently in football, could cause a sudden jab of pain, momentarily resulting in reflex release of the ball. If this happened while Nick was carrying the ball, the result could be a disaster for the team. Better not to chance it. Nick did not play.

There was a somewhat similar situation in a game, probably in my first year with the team. I had injected a small area of the foot of Billie Gay, one of our best halfbacks. He had good relief of the pain where he had probably suffered a minor tear of the tough bands of tissue beneath the skin at the sole of the foot. He played well for a while, but then he experienced a sudden severe pain in that area of his foot as he was running with the ball. He dropped to the ground in pain—ending his run, which could have been for a touchdown. Apparently, the anesthetic had worn off and the sudden stretching of the fascial bands as he ran caused more pain and possibly more injury. Although there was no serious consequence to the foot, there was drama on the field to see a man in pain and a spectacular run spoiled. He was taken out of the game.

On occasions our decisions to keep a man out of play was unpopular with the coach. He could reason that the doctor was too cautious, or that he did not understand the importance of getting that man back on the field. Some coaches appeared to have become accustomed to other practices elsewhere whereby they were able to influence medical decisions. The care that the athletes deserved was just then becoming established.

I learned early in the course of my work there that taking care of these athletes differed considerably from the usual medical practice. The Head Coach was the central figure in this picture, and it was he who bore the burden of managing the football team of men and boys—a hundred and more—of the caliber expected at ND. The Coach held total control of this picture and it could make the doctor's work difficult when the ambitions of the coach interfered with the care of the injured player. This observation was well exemplified by an early experience with Coach Leahy, shortly after I began my involvement with Notre Dame.

It was only the second week of pre-season football practice in the fall of 1949 at the University of Notre Dame. One of the varsity football players, Frank Rodney Johnston, showed up that day at the student infirmary where I saw patients a few days of the week. He had suffered an injury to his knee and was unable to practice. The injury was almost a week old. Rodney walked into the infirmary limping badly. My examination showed a swollen knee, tense with fluid, painful, and tender medially. Stressing the knee to evaluate the ligaments revealed instability of the medial structures and laxity of the anterior cruciate ligament, the ACL.

The trainers had advised Rodney to see me a week earlier. He had reluctantly put it off until now, when he saw that this was not going to be well in a few days or a week. X-rays of the knee had been taken and were normal, leading to a false impression of the nature of that injury.

This was 1949. The science of sports medicine was early in its evolution. Primitive as it seems today, the accepted treatment of that injury to the medial structures and the ACL at the time was to put the parts to rest and allow the ligaments to heal as best they could. Casts were recommended to insure rest, healing, and comfort. That was the "state of the art."

On explaining the full nature of the injury, and in keeping with the currently accepted teaching, I persuaded Rodney that the right thing to do would be to put it at rest to allow the torn structures to heal. Rodney agreed. I aspirated about a half cup of blood from the joint, applied a cast, and put him on crutches.

Rodney went out to practice and reported to the trainer, Hugh Burns, who told Rodney that he had better report to the coach as well, which he did. (Rodney loved to tell this story in later years when we had become good friends. He told it with Leahy's manner and voice.)

Rodney hobbled out onto the practice field on crutches and walked up behind Coach Leahy. Rodney addressed him: "Coach," he said. Coach Leahy turned around and looked Rodney over.

It was then that Leahy asked in his quiet and masterful way, "Oh, Rodney. What is that on your leg?" On hearing the answer, the coach delivered his diatribe. He said, "Oh, Rodney, you go right back to those doctors and tell them to take that off your leg. Those doctors are alarmists. They would put a cast on a pimple.

Get that off your leg right now. You go back to those doctors. Tell them to take that thing off your leg."

Rodney limped away but, instead of returning to the infirmary where he knew what the answer would be, he went home to Cincinnati where his friendly family doctor obliged his request and removed the cast.

Rodney checked in with the trainers and was back in his position several weeks later, playing with a tight wrap on his knee. I had not yet developed the closeness of working with the trainers and so I didn't catch up with this for those weeks.

When I did, I spoke to the trainers who reluctantly explained how their jobs depended on following the coach's orders, and they were following orders. They had rehabilitated Rodney to the point where he could return to play his position as left guard with a good strapping on the still-swollen knee.

I was rather new on my job, only a few weeks into it, and I didn't really know how far my authority extended in matters such as this.

Dr. Sherman Egan, an internist, was the recently appointed Director of the medical affairs of the University. He and I discussed the situation, including the lack of compliance with the advised medical care of Rodney, and its medico-legal aspects. Since the medical department and medical team continued to have a responsibility in these cases, we decided to present our dilemma to Father Joyce, who was Chairman of the Faculty Board of Athletics. He understood the problem only too well—the authoritarianism of the head coach. Father Joyce took immediate action. His word was passed down to Moose Krause, the Athletic Director, and then to Coach Leahy. It was to be understood by all that this was a medical problem under the care of the physicians, and the physicians' advice was to be followed. Father Joyce established that ruling and it was observed. There were occasional differences with this by various coaches over the years, but Father Joyce always backed us up in such situations.

Coach Leahy reluctantly accepted this understanding. He had his own ideas of how the program, which he viewed as his program, was to be run. He occupied a commanding position at the University, having previously established his reputation in the field of sports. The prominence of football in the history and traditions of the school were such that his mastery of football at Notre Dame appeared to put him above reproach. This attitude surfaced again at a later date.

Bill Barrett, prized halfback of 1950, was injured early in the fall of the following year. He suffered an apparent ankle sprain. The original X-rays were normal but the ankle was very swollen. He was seen by the physician at the student infirmary and was referred to the trainers. These men had cared for many sprained ankles. They started him on physical therapy. They put him through their usual treatments of alternating warm and cold immersions, whirlpool, and assisted active exercise. They were now into massage and forced passive motion, only to find the ankle becoming worse, still swollen, and tender. Motion was limited.

Bill was now referred to me. We had further X-rays, which now revealed calcification developing in the area between the tibia and the fibula, the two long bones of the leg, which formed the ankle mortise. This was a more severe degree of injury than the usual sprained ankle. This was another situation that required rest to prevent further spread of the calcification, allowing it to mature, and with hopes that the condition then would be more manageable. A cast was applied.

Bill was a very important element in Leahy's plans for the year. His best rusher—in a cast! He could not play in a cast. It was soon removed. I learned of this and advised Billie to allow me to reapply the cast. Billie rejected the advice. Therapy was resumed with little benefit. After graduation, he had some surgery in Chicago, but he did not play football again. A good player was lost. Leahy continued to build his program his way.

Early Trainers

IN THOSE DAYS, the coach's word was law. The treatment of injuries in times past was a somewhat difficult problem. Coaches were often reluctant to have their player see a doctor. The coaches sometimes took medical situations into their own hands, or otherwise they relied on the trainers to administer medical care.

In these earlier days, a trainer had little formal training. His background might be that of administering first aid at an industrial plant or, having been an athlete himself in earlier days, someone who felt capable of dealing with the injuries of the team in the same way that he had been treated. A roll of tape, some Ace bandages, dressings, a bandage scissors, a bottle of iodine, and "smelling salts" were the trainer's usual equipment. Treatment usually consisted of the application of heat or cold, and rubdowns and massage with alcohol and liniments. The trainers did, however, have a lot of practical knowledge and cared for the athlete as best they could, enabling many a grateful man to return to play.

The trainers themselves were highly experienced in looking after the routine injuries, painful and severe though they might be. They would have the usual sprained ankle back in play, with a good strapping, in ten days or so. Most of us would still be limping several weeks after such a sprained ankle. The players and the team could not afford that luxury. The athletes wanted to get back into the action, and the coach wanted them back too.

The early trainers did not have the advantage of modern training facilities. Initially the trainer's domain at Notre Dame was a room in a corner under the stadium housing a couple of

Our trainer, Gene Paszkiet, administers "smelling salts" to Dave Flood for a concussion, the usual routine at that time.

whirlpools, a diathermy, and several examining tables. During those years, we did not have a weight room. The athletes used other types of activities to strengthen their muscles: free weights; weighted sleds to be pushed around; the lifting of heavy objects such as tractor tires; or isometrics, such as Al Ecuyer is reported to have used—pushing his head and neck against a wall with maximal exertion. (The muscles of his neck were developed to the point at which the width of his neck was virtually that of his head.)

The more determined and resourceful athletes found the opportunity for serious weightlifting workouts in Father Lange's gym. Father was an old-time weightlifter, having captured several titles in that sport before he entered the priesthood. He continued to lift to preserve his strength as well as he could. He was a rather cantankerous old priest. He might agree to let certain athletes use his equipment if they were there to work—no fooling around! If he saw that they were not serious in lifting, that was it. They were out. Father Lange did get results.

Eventually, we had our own treatment room, as well as a grandiose training area, complete with mirrored walls, enabling the athletes to pose and admire their developing physiques. The room was outfitted with free weights, as well as the most modern resistance equipment to assist injured players in their recovery and for the development of the brute strength of these athletes. The weight trainer supervised and developed routines for them.

One of the earliest trainers of record at Notre Dame, O.H. Glimstedt, G.D., did this work on a part-time basis, teaching at the University at the same time. He wrote a small handbook sometime prior to 1930 on the treatment of athletic injuries, one of the earliest publications on the subject known to me. This publication was sponsored by the makers of "Antiphlogistine," a medical ointment purported to be very beneficial in the massage of athletic injuries. The author wrote extensively on massage and he probably used a lot of the ointment.

Glimstedt pointed out the danger of coaches taking over the medical care of their athletes. This was the practice at some schools whereby the coach and his trainer gave medical care to their athlete, avoiding doctors who so often ruled the player out of athletics. He had other advice. Goose grease was his preference in massage after workouts to prevent "colds" in the sweating athlete. He also advised that players with venereal diseases—"the unclean"—should not share the bathing facilities with the other players. The trainers took care of all the medical problems.

Another of the early trainers at the school was "Scrap-iron" Young. He was there from 1930 to 1944. He must have had an engaging personality to compensate for his minimal training, whatever that had been. He had a good following of athletes and nonprofessionals, at least until he unfortunately found himself treating a painful condition about the shoulder of one of our citizens as he would treat any painful state, only to learn in time that there was an underlying malignancy. Soon thereafter, the school found another trainer.

By the time I entered the sports medicine scene in 1949, trainers were far more competent. Several colleges and universities now had courses of study that applied to their work. There were courses in anatomy, physiology, kinesiology, first aid, taping and bracing, etc., which would help trainers in their profession. Not long after that, colleges began offering a curriculum designed for trainers, leading to a college degree in their field.

In 1952, the National Athletic Trainers Association (N.A.T.A.) was organized. This association prescribed courses of study and programs for trainers. Soon thereafter, the American Physical

Therapy Association (A.P.T.A.) entered the field, requiring even more advanced studies for qualification as a trainer. These organizations conducted educational programs to keep trainers abreast of medical advances in the area of their work, including refresher courses and examinations to qualify them as trainers. All of these developments resulted in better-trained men.

Notre Dame Trainers

HUGH BURNS became the head trainer at Notre Dame in 1945 and was there when I first started. He probably had some formal training. He knew enough to keep his athletes going and generally kept the coaches happy. Gene Paszkiet was a certified head trainer from 1952 to 1979. He worked with me during most of my years at ND. John Whitmer, who was his assistant, became head trainer thereafter. Jim Russ was head trainer when I finished at Notre Dame. He and Rod Hunt, the current head trainer, were well-trained men who were fully trained and certified as Athletic Trainers. There were also student trainers in the department working with these men as part of their scholarship work requirements.

"Skip" Meyer, also certified, was trainer for the basketball team and had the all-important job of placating the coach, "Digger" Phelps, who was a very independent man and could be quite demanding. He had only a handful of men, so he was eager to keep all of them healthy.

I worked closely with the trainers. They were practical men and did their work well. It was important that they recognize those conditions requiring the direction of a physician, while they performed those services of which they felt capable. Since they were closer to the players, they came to know their athletes well over a period of time, and they also came to know the forces—psychological and others—which drove them. They knew the temperaments of the various athletes. The trainers were psychologists in their own right in many cases, as were the coaches.

This information was necessary also for my understanding and management of an individual's complaints. Gene Paszkiet, the trainer with whom I worked for the major part of my time with the team, made an interesting observation one day. He agreed it did not hold true in all cases, but he felt that he had to have his running backs feel their very best, like racehorses, to function well. On the other hand, I recalled what Coach John Ray had said in his hoarse voice, "Doc, linemen play with injuries." And they did. They took a beating on every play. Pain and soreness were their lot.

Caring for these players meant more than taking care of their injuries or complaints. At times, this meant identifying the player who preferred to minimize a problem so he would not miss play, in contrast to the player who avoided practice while being treated in the training room most of the week, but was ready to play on game day. Both of these players would be eager to play. The first could be apprehensive that another player might take over his hard-earned position. The second man was secure in his position, but he just didn't like the rigors of practice.

It was as important to understand this in these young men as it was to understand the workings of the mind of the wealthy dowager I might see in the office. Gene and the other head trainers came to know their players well, and this information was passed on to me when I saw these men. It was of help in managing their care.

It was our job to see that these men received proper medical care and to get them back to play as soon as possible and safely. This is a particular area in which the management of an injured patient varied from that of the casual patient seen in the office for the

The author, Dr. Les Bodnar, walks on the field with trainer Gene Paszkiet on his right as the game is about to start.

same injury. Fortunately, these young men were almost universally eager to return to activity. Not necessarily so in my office practice, especially if the complaint was work related. That was the "fun" part of the medical job with the athletes. Here, there was less hassle. They helped you get them well. They made you look good.

Official Duties

MY FIRST OFFICIAL duty with the head trainer and the University physician that fall—and each fall thereafter for the next 34 years— would be the preseason examination of the new and returning members of the team, and those student athletes who decided to "walk on," hoping to make the team.

The first group we examined each fall was a group of players, about forty or more, consisting mostly of freshmen, including those athletes on scholarships. The new men were given a more detailed general physical examination since these men had never been examined for our program prior to their arrival. With the help of physicians and dentists from the South Bend community, an assembly line of stations was set up in the training room for the various specialists to perform their exams, pro-bono. These professionals were glad to be part of the program, to be identified with the team. For many years, Dr. George Green, who was designated as "team doctor," was the general surgeon checking for hernias and whatever else came under his specialty. Dentists, Drs. Jack Stenger and Ed Lawton, made molds for the protective mouth-guards, which would be made individually to fit each man who passed the examinations. Various ENT men, such as Drs. Steve McTigue and Bryan Saine, would conduct their ENT exams. Drs. Howard Engel and Steve Anderson were often the internists checking the hearts and lungs of these aspiring young men. I would do the orthopaedic exams, evaluating any abnormalities with my colleagues. There were several other orthopaedic surgeons associated with the overall program. Initially, Dr. Marlin Troyer assisted. Later my other associates, Drs. Will Yergler and David Bankoff, worked with me. These men covered this and other aspects of the program, including the play and practice sessions of the varsity teams.

The incoming players were generally in good shape after a summer program of conditioning, hardening them for the strenuous workouts ahead of them during that fall period. Yet, especially with the newcomers, there were often problems to be worked out.

There were several years when a few of the recruits came

in with injuries, occasionally serious—such as to the ligaments of the knee—after having played in high school all-star games during the summer season. These injuries were still fresh, so we could take care of those. Sometimes other problems arose, which required decisions that were more complicated.

I recall the dilemma we envisioned when one new man appeared with severe hearing loss. How did he get into the lineup? And how could he play? He couldn't hear the signals, the quarterback's count, or the referee's whistle. Surprisingly he managed. He made the squad as a defensive lineman entering the play with the snap

Mike Oriard walked on and became our starting center at ND. He then played professionally. He is now a professor teaching at Oregon State University.

of the ball. Unfortunately, he had a knee injury, which limited his ability to play. He transferred to another school the next year.

Among the freshmen athletes we examined, there were always a number of ambitious walk-ons, boys who had made their mark in high school football but had not been offered scholarships. One of these was Mike Oriard who walked on, made the varsity, and was center for the team during his junior and senior years. Mike was an exceptional individual, captain of the team his senior year, with a 4.0 grade point average scholastically for his four years at Notre Dame. He then proceeded into the professional ranks, playing with Kansas City from 1970-74. He continued his education, earning his PhD at Stanford. Thereafter he entered the teaching profession and became a college professor, which he is today at Oregon State University.

Success among walk-ons such as Mike Oriard continues to inspire these young hopefuls, some of whom do make the grade to varsity. They continue to dream of playing at ND. And some do have the ability to do so, but the chances of their beating out a scholarship player are slim. They would indeed be lucky to be discovered amidst the goodly number of ball players aspiring to have the opportunity to play for ND.

Nevertheless, there was an occasional player on the inter-hall teams who was "discovered" with the talent and the work ethic to make the varsity roster. Over the years, there were several punters and kickers and a few players at other positions who were successful in gaining varsity status. Such was the case with both Chuck Male (1978) and Reggie Ho (1988) who were found playing inter-hall football when the team needed a better kicker.

Another player from the inter-hall ranks of football players was Pat Heenan in 1959. He played inter-hall football for three years and then went out for the varsity his senior year. He not only made the team as an end, but he also continued into the pro ranks after graduation and played for the Washington Redskins.

In the usual routines, walk-ons and the less talented players are relegated to the "prep" squads or are dropped from the team. All of us know one of those prep players, also a "walk-on" who became an icon for today's group of aspiring players. It was Daniel "Rudy" Ruettiger, better known simply as "Rudy," who gained fame for his toughness and perseverance while practicing with the varsity. He ultimately made the game-day roster and finally entered the last game of the season for the one play that made his fame, even to the extent of having a movie made of his career at ND. His story was dramatic and a credit to him. Even today, in Notre Dame circles, Rudy's name is famous. This gave reason for all to remain hopeful.

The next day we examined the returning varsity players. They were carefully checked on old injuries, some from the prior season, or other conditions they may have incurred over the summer.

There were always a few problems amongst this returning group. I remember the unusual sight of Vegas Ferguson returning one fall, bent over like an old man, unable to stand erectly. Our best running back! What happened? What was this about? Were we to lose this prime player? Instead, he proved to be such a gung-ho pre-season conditioning enthusiast that he had performed a hundred and more sit-ups the day before, straining his abdominal muscles, probably suffering micro-tears of some fibers, as a result of which they were so sore that he could not extend his body fully. He couldn't stand erect without pain. Fortunately, with treatment by our trainers, this wore off within a few days, to the relief of everyone concerned.

More often, the problem was not that simple. Ian Gray, a tackle on defense, was one of these. He had been working on a summer job in a factory, operating machinery and had looked away from his work momentarily. The press came down on his hand, crushing three fingers, causing compound fractures. The injuries had healed by the fall but the finger joints did not have full motion and required protection. They could easily be reinjured by direct contact. We had a plastic brace fabricated to protect the hand. That enabled him to participate fully in play.

Steve Quehl was not as fortunate. A truck he was operating that summer had virtually blown up beneath him. He was not fit to play that year but was our center in 1975.

A heart-wrenching case was that of Don Hogan, a very highly talented halfback from the Chicago area who had proven himself as a player. He had been the leading runner on the 1962 Notre Dame Varsity Team. As a sophomore, he had rushed for 330 yards in 88 plays. He had been seriously injured in an automobile accident early in 1963. He had suffered severe fractures of his pelvis and hip. He recovered and was released by his doctors to play football that fall.

However, my exam revealed limitation of hip motions and X-rays revealed abnormalities of the socket of the hip joint. That hip would never be within the functional levels required for athletic competition. Moreover, it was even more likely that the condition would be materially worsened by participating in a rugged game. There was a lot of pressure to have him play, especially since he had been such an outstanding player up to that time. With everyone fully aware and with pressure from all sides—coaches, parents, and the boy—I agreed to a compromise, a trial of function. The parents and the player fully understood the possibilities, which I have stated. He would nevertheless be allowed to "try out" with the team, and he did. He wanted so badly to play, and so did everyone else, but within the first weeks, the hip had become painful and dysfunctional, leading to his realization that he would not be playing again. The coaching staff arranged for him to do assistant coaching, giving him some satisfaction, just to stay with the game and to be part of the Notre Dame family. He kept his scholarship, but the physical pain had been too much for him. The emotional pain was probably just as great, if not more so. This arrangement was somewhat of a balm to him.

One year a very determined freshman presented for examination. He was a man of proven ability, with an enviable record as a running back in high school football. He showed up with a knee injury incurred the prior season. The knee was grossly unstable; he had suffered tears of the anterior cruciate ligament and extensive tearing of the medial structures of the joint. The state of the art at that time was such that I could not promise him nor the coaches that surgical reconstruction of the joint would offer a reasonable chance to enable the player to participate in big-time football. This was not a fresh injury, which would have had high potential for a good result with the good healing qualities of a fresh injury. To reconstruct was not the same as operating on freshly torn structures that still had the potential for good healing. The methods advocated for such a knee at that time were not yet advanced to the point at which the knee would be within a few millimeters of normal stability on stress testing the ligaments, which would probably then have allowed him to play, with adequate muscle strengthening and bracing, without undue risk of re-injury. I disqualified him. He would retain his scholarship, but he would not be part of the football program.

This did not set well with the boy and his family. He was still eager to play but his knee was very unstable. The ligaments had been torn and, with that knee, he was subject to be easily re-injured, a disadvantage to himself and the team. He was vulnerable.

He would be a liability. I disqualified him despite the objections raised by the young man and his family. They used what pressure they could on me, the coaches, and the authorities at Notre Dame. When this failed to gain his entry, they went to the NCAA. An investigation supported my position and the complaint eventually died. I heard that he was admitted to the football program at another school, but I never heard of him thereafter.

The results of these pre-season exams were always a concern to the coaches and medical staff. In this group of select young men, there were few disappointments, but they did occur from time to time, and these players had to be weeded out. This was for the good of the aspiring athlete, as well as for the program, but that was not easy to accept when you were the one to be refused entry into the program, when your one thought had been that you had at last achieved your goal.

On the Job

HUGH BURNS, the Head Trainer, and I first met with the beginning of the fall football program in 1949. He was a very affable and capable fellow whose training was on a par with the general group of trainers of that day—minimal formal training, but plenty of practical knowledge.

It was in the month of August. The fall football workouts had started. There would be a few weeks of pre-season training before the first game. There had been no formal or organized practice until then, according to the rules. However, there were always a few players going to summer school who might get together on occasion, maybe even every day, and throw the ball around, and maybe there could be a coach somewhere observing this, and who knows how many more maybe's there might be. This was a common practice among teams, to get "one up" on their opponents.

Hugh Burns called me one day in those first weeks of preseason practice asking me to come by to see one of the athletes at the end of my office hours. The school term had not yet started. I went out to the training room. Hughie showed me around. It was on that occasion that I met Leon Hart for the first time. He had already established his reputation for his toughness and abilities in the line, an end, playing on offense and defense, as players did in those days. He was also an occasional fullback. He was to become the Heisman Trophy winner that year.

Hugh proudly showed me his method of adding support to Leon's knee. It had been injured a few weeks earlier and was still tender and swollen along its medial aspect. I tested the medial collateral ligament. There was a suggestion of slight instability, a minor tear of the ligament, now several weeks old.

Hugh had taped a four-inch-wide piece of automobile tire inner tubing about fourteen-inches long, spanning the joint in hope of adding to the stability of that side of the knee. Leon was preparing to go to practice with this on his leg, as he had been doing for the last few weeks. Leon insisted that the knee felt fine and that he was able to play "as good as ever" with this support. I left well enough alone. There was nothing more to be done since the muscles of the leg remained strong. With further experience, I realized that this slight, two or three mm excess laxity on stressing of the ligaments was compatible with good function when the muscles crossing the joint were trained to a high level of strength. Hughie's approach to the problem was novel, but it worked.

An Away Game

HUGH BURNS worked hard to include me in the team the first year and to make me comfortable behind the scenes in this strange new world of college athletics. This medical "team" included the trainer and me, as well as the University physician, and the team physician, Dr. George Green.

In 1949, several weeks into the fall schedule, Hughie suggested that I should go along with the team to the Michigan State Game. This would be with the official party, which included my wife. It seemed that it should be a nice experience, and so we went.

The trip was by train. The team, its entourage, and official party had two Pullman coaches and a dining car. The remainder of the train consisted of about eight coaches of happy and exuberant alumni and fans.

The train pulled out of the downtown station of South Bend. The dining car opened soon after we left the station, and they started feeding the players. It was axiomatic at that time that these young men should eat a heavy diet of red meat before the game to give them strength and vigor. So steak and potatoes it was—a nice sirloin, a little bigger than your hand and wrist, almost an inch thick—a real meal for real men. My wife Bunny and I were served the same.

We had seated ourselves in the dining car at a table with Julius Tucker. Julius was a businessman who had several successful businesses. He was a close friend to Coach Leahy and was a "regular" in the locker room and around the team. He knew the players and the seniors especially knew him. Julius advised them, and without involving himself financially, he arranged contracts for the athletes with various professional football teams. He did not profit from this; it was a hobby or a sideline for him. He had

Paul Burns, a guard on the 1949 team

especially close contact with the Chicago Bears, as well as good connections with other professional football teams.

Julius was toying with his steak when Paul Burns, middle noseguard on the team, sauntered over and sat down with us. Paul had finished his steak. Then, as if by a routine previously established, Julius offered his steak to Paul. The second steak went down as fast as the first one, to the appreciation of Paul

Burns. We did not have dieticians in those days. They would never have approved of this. He played well the entire game. He was not slowed by two steaks for the pre-game meal.

It was several years later before the dieticians and nutritionists persuaded the coaches that less protein and more carbs were a better diet the night before the game. Furthermore, the players were encouraged to eat what they chose to eat under normal conditions. That might vary from a "Danish" to scrambled eggs and sausage before the game. There is indeed a great difference in the eating habits of people. This arrangement today suits everyone and does better in ensuring a proper pre-game meal to everyone's satisfaction.

The fans had brought loads of food and iced beer aboard. A favorite local restaurant, Alby's, cemented its following by providing loads of fried chicken. It wasn't long before the alumni and fans had the train rocking to the music of the accordion and gut bucket which had been brought aboard. In no time, we heard the discordant voices of the crowd on the train, singing, whooping and cheering to the tunes of Notre Dame songs or dancing to the raucous sounds of the "Beer Barrel Polka." Most of the fans became happier and happier, while the others became more and more disgusted with the display of rowdiness and drunkenness of their fellow travelers. It wasn't surprising that some of those happiest revelers didn't bother to get off the train when we arrived in Lansing—nor were they capable of doing so.

The train pulled into an area not far from the stadium. We walked over, my wife going into the stands with the official party. We, the medical staff and the team and coaches, arrived at the stadium and entered our locker room. It was a large, clean, and spacious room with adjacent shower and bathroom facilities. There were benches and lockers along the sides, a small isolated room in the corner for the trainer, and another room for the coaches.

The players walked in rather quietly, surveyed the room, found their lockers, and went about their routine preparations for the game. They prepared for the game in a businesslike way, talking quietly as they dressed for the game. The student managers had set out the uniforms at the lockers assigned to specific players, grouping them by their playing positions. The assistant coaches moved amongst their men who were thus grouped, giving them last-minute advice and encouragement. Hugh Burns and his student trainers were busy strapping ankles and various other joints, and checking on gear of various kinds where extra support was necessary for protection, mainly for old injuries. When the players were ready, they relaxed on blankets on the floor or sat around chatting or psyching themselves up for the game.

At a given signal from the field, the players began exiting the room in a preordained manner, with successive groups leaving the room to begin their calisthenics and warm-up drills on the field.

Hugh encouraged me to go out on the field with them, which I did. It is always a bit awesome to walk out onto the field, with thousands of people filtering into the stands, with the bands playing, the crowd's noise ringing in your ears, listening to their cheers, jeers, and boastful banter, while greeting the usual sideline aficionados. Meanwhile, I was also watchful, dodging the players racing by to get a ball that just missed my head.

That scene always raised your pulse a bit, less so with more experience, and little more even when the game started. There is a sense of self-consciousness too at first, but that leaves once the game starts.

After a good interval, during which the players followed a set routine in preparation for the game itself, they completed their general warm-up. At a given signal, we all ran back to the locker room.

The players did their little personal things now while they waited to start the game. Maybe a tape job needed reinforcement. Some just sat and stared at their feet. One more trip to the john. I'm sure some said their personal prayers. One sat and jiggled one knee up and down, then the other knee, then both knees, getting rid of his nervous tension. And then came the call: "Five more minutes, Coach!"

Coach Leahy called for their attention. He spoke of them as "lads" and addressed them as such. At other times, he addressed them as "gentlemen." He spoke firmly and directly to them, reminding them of the importance of this game, the hard work they had endured in preparation for it, the need for each man to perform his role on that field to perfection, and how each man's teammates were depending on him. He spoke of the pride Notre Dame felt in them, and of the wonderful opportunity that lay before them to win a game for Notre Dame, for the glory of Our Lady's School. He spoke of them as "the best." He then turned to our priest. We all knelt. The priest said a prayer, asking for God's blessing and safekeeping. With the "Amen" they gave a whoop and a holler and a "Let's go" and filed out of the room. Some, more religious than others, received individual blessings from the priest, then ran out through the tunnel and onto the field to the roar of the crowd.

The coach was the last to leave. As he came to the door, I shook his hand and wished him good luck. He turned to me, looking me straight in the eye, and said, very seriously, "Thank you, doctor." I still remember the words, the tone, the firm look in his eyes and the firm handshake.

Now those three little words from the Coach may not mean much to some, but it was said in such a serious and meaningful way that I can still feel the power of the man as he said it. His words must have had the same effect on his players and others. Some men have that ability, to lead men, to instill confidence, to persuade them of the need to devote themselves to the job at hand, to give it their utmost effort. Regardless of any faults he might have had, Coach Leahy did have that charisma.

On the field, the men went through a quick "warm-up" drill, then a few preliminary plays to hone their skills, and then they were ready. The officials went to the middle of the field to meet with the team captains. They went through the coin toss and the choosing of sides. Then the captains shook hands—a show of good sportsmanship—and returned to their respective sidelines and teammates.

At the last second, our players all gathered around the Coach. The players huddled close as he gave them some last-minute words of encouragement. The referees blew a whistle. The team then dispersed to the field or the sidelines, whatever their role, taking their positions. We, the medical staff, retired to the sidelines.

Now with both teams on the field, the game started and the battle was on. The first half was hard fought. Michigan State always presented a well-prepared and capable team. Their coach, "Biggie" Munn, was a well-established and successful coach. His easygoing personality could easily disarm you. On guard! He was smart, canny, and had good and well-coached personnel. It could be a serious error to underrate him or his team.

Michigan State and Notre Dame had a history of intense rivalry. These were always hard fought games. Midway into the first quarter, fear suddenly seized me. Larry Coutre, one of our halfbacks, had run the ball and, as he was hit, he went heels over head and came down on his head and neck. He lay there for a moment, not moving. Another few seconds and he was up.

Apparently he had been stunned momentarily, but not injured. I breathed more easily. When I saw the play as it occurred, I could imagine that his neck was broken. I thought of the possibility of the total paralysis that might occur. Thank God it wasn't any of that. I was amazed then and many more times in the future of the resiliency of the human body.

The first half ended just after Dave Flood, our right halfback, came out of the game, his one arm dangling loosely, somewhat supported by his other arm, and in pain. I had seen this before, typical of a fractured collarbone. We helped him to the training room. The first half ended.

At halftime, the team crowded into the locker room. The managers had spread blankets on the floor so the players could relax there. Slices of oranges had been prepared and laid out for them to replenish their energies. They needed fluid, water, plenty of it. They soon began to talk, a little bantering, talking to each other of their play, kidding each other a bit, but still serious and exhibiting the tension of men who have yet to finish a job.

I examined Dave further in the locker room. The fracture was the usual one, through the middle third of the clavicle. There was no suggestion of further complication from it. The treatment was easy. In the locker room, I padded the axillae and used a "figure eight" shoulder strapping, retracting the shoulders to align the fragments of the clavicle and to restrict movement of the parts. Dave was given a mild sedative. He later returned to the sidelines for the rest of the game.

The coach had been observing me while I took care of Dave. He must have been satisfied that I knew what I was doing and had done it with dispatch, since I had the sense that he regarded me somewhat differently now—more like a doctor, not another "hanger-on." This was a late-developing perception by the coach, leading to some degree of confidence with which the coach now viewed my position. His confidence was necessary in working with him and with the team.

The coaches gathered in their room, discussed the course of the game, what was working, what wasn't, the opponent's strategies, and means of counterattacking them, changing game plans, if and when necessary. They then came out and went to their respective groups of players, informing them of any changes in tactics and giving other advice and information to the players to help them in the second half of the game. By now, it was time to go back onto the field, and out they went.

The game continued without any real disasters thereafter, but that is not to say there was anything easy about the play. There were a good number of lesser injuries to be evaluated the next day at the Sunday morning clinic.

On that day, we beat Michigan State 34-21. After the game, there was loud and gusty exuberance, shouting and talking in the locker room among the valiant warriors. They showered, dressed, and went out to meet their parents, girlfriends, and well-wishers, engaging in light-hearted conversations until it came time to get back on the train. The return trip was not as raucous. Tired and sleepy players and fans, all depleted of their energies and some, in the case of fans, groggy with alcohol, were all glad to rest, to call it a day. Then back to campus where a group of loyal "Domers" hailed the team, prior to whisking many of them off to a more beery reception elsewhere. The "walking wounded" would appear at my clinic the next morning. Dave Flood was taken to the student infirmary.

A Career in Sports Medicine

MY WORK WITH NOTRE DAME would prove to be an interesting diversion in a world different from that to which I was accustomed. It also had its more difficult aspects. The major part of the job was the care of the students, not those on the athletic teams. The entire student body, it seemed, was involved in sports and games, including the inter-hall athletic programs, which included football and basketball. These sports caused most of the athletic injuries. This included varsity and inter-hall football, as well as pick-up games of "touch" football; varsity basketball, and the ongoing on-campus games of basketball, terminating in the perennial Bookstore Basketball Tournament. These games resulted in diverse injuries, mostly to the wrists, knees, and ankles.

The other sports also had their injuries, with certain ones being the most characteristic of certain sports: ankle sprains and basketball went together; overuse caused shoulder pain in baseball, swimming, and tennis; track brought foot disorders; tennis and baseball players had elbow problems; hockey players banged and separated shoulder joints; and fencers suffered knee problems. All the other sports also contributed to the total gamut of afflictions that were referred to my attention.

Many of the injuries were rather routine and were weeded out by the physician who saw them in the infirmary. The more serious injuries were referred to my attention. Those suffered by the varsity athletes were seen by the trainers. The trainers knew these injuries and the management of them well, and they kept us, the medical staff, informed, and consulted us when necessary. They knew which athletes deserved X-ray studies and which should be referred to the physician. At times, the acute and severe injuries required my immediate attention. At other times, the chronic nagging conditions were a problem to all of us. The trainers were a great help to me. They were able to guide me through the routines while I was learning this aspect of my work.

The Bengal Bouts were one of the student activities requiring a physician at ringside. This was a boxing event, a series of bouts for a group of students who had been training for months and had been paired off by weight and skill by the longtime director of the program, Dominic Napolitano. The bouts were an ND tradition held for the benefit of the Bengal Missions of the Congregation of Holy Cross. The fights were of three short rounds officiated by big-time referees, timekeepers, and judges.

It was part of my work to be the doctor at ringside for these fights. In the early days, the bouts were held in the old Fieldhouse. It was filled to overflowing for the "Bengals." On one of these occasions, the bouts were the finals of the progressive elimination bouts of the past few weeks. I recall the intense argument I had with the brother of a boxer in these Bengal Bouts. The fighter under discussion had fought his way to the finals and was known to be a good boxer. He was scheduled for one of the championship bouts. However, in his preliminary fight a few days earlier, he had suffered a facial laceration requiring sutures, and the sutures were still in his face. I couldn't approve him. The fighter and his brother argued that the fighter was good at protecting himself. They were sure he would not be hurt. I should not worry about that cut, even though I knew that a blow to the laceration would tear it open, complicating the injury, probably causing more scarring of the face, a bloody mess in the ring, and censure of all on the scene. I had to make that decision, to the great disappointment of the boxer and his brother. They both felt that I had cheated the boxer of a glorious victory. There is a chance that I did; but I also did him a favor and a barbaric bloody scene was probably avoided.

Another episode that involved a boxer in the Bengals was that of one of the fighters whose shoulder dislocated as he threw a heavy punch. I was at ringside as he dropped into the familiar posture that I had seen many times before, of standing semi-flexed while supporting the dangling arm with the other hand. The referee stopped the fight. I jumped into the ring and was trying to guide the boxer out of the ring when he stopped and told me: "Just put it in, Doc." He relaxed his muscles as I told him to do and, sure enough, the shoulder slipped right back in with a little traction. Still trying to get him out of the ring, he stopped me and said, "I'm okay, Doc.

It happens in other sports too. Here, Bill Hanzlik is playing basketball while wearing a nose guard after having suffered a fractured nasal bone, which required reduction and protection.

I've had it out a lot of times. I can finish the fight." By now, he was waving the arm all about, but I noticed that he avoided that particular motion which was likely to cause it to dislocate again. He was very persuasive. I talked with the referee and we decided to allow the bout to continue. I don't really recall whether he won or lost; but it was an example of determination, "guts," toughness, and disregard of pain to achieve that goal toward which he had worked so hard.

Toughness of this kind was not uncommon in these athletes. I recall an early fall game with Southern Cal in South Bend in the days before face masks were part of the usual protective equipment worn by players. Collision with an opponent's helmet had created a bloody gash over Walt Grothaus's cheekbone. A few minutes of pressure quickly stopped the bleeding. With the bleeding controlled, we went out through the tunnel at the north end of the field to the ambulance parked there. It whisked us to the infirmary where I sewed him up under local anesthesia, just as we did so many times to those tough hockey players, who frequently suffered these lacerations. Back we went to the stadium. He was ready to go in the second half of the game—this time with a protective facemask—but the game was now nearly over so he did not get back into the game.

Pete Duranko also showed his toughness when he came down hard on the side of one foot, twisting his ankle severely. He barely managed to get off the field. He sat on the bench sweating and cursing his fortunes. The ankle was tender, starting to swell, and painful with motion. I looked at the ankle with Gene Paszkiet who was trainer at the time. Pete was foully scolding his fates. He told Gene, "Fix it up, Gene. The ankle's okay. Just wrap it up good. Make it tight. I gotta get back in the game." I was satisfied that this was not a fracture. Gene wrapped the foot and ankle tightly, and Duranko was back in the game. The crowd in the stands was unaware of the injury and the determined toughness of a guy like this. Even with some limitation of his ability to play, he was still one of the best for his position at that time.

Willie Fry was another case in point. In the 1973 game against Boston College, Willie suffered a broken nose, bloody but straight. He was a big man, powerful, a smart player, and stoic—a defensive end. The bleeding soon stopped. We went to the locker room. I fashioned a facemask of heat malleable plastic, essentially a nose guard, flaring out over his cheeks and forehead. He was back in the game in the second half. His play was essential to that win. He tolerated whatever pain he might have been having rather than miss play. This may seem barbaric to those unfamiliar with sports at this level, but the athletes have accepted this as part of the game.

It's not that these men are immune to pain. They do have a higher tolerance and have learned to ignore the pain with the help of the adrenaline rush and their natural endorphins binding to certain receptors in the brain, releasing dopamine, which mitigates the pain to a level tolerable for the player in these intensely competitive moments. Their brains are programmed to disregard pain of this degree. Boxers do the same. These are part of our primitive responses to danger, to pain, and for survival.

Protecting the Athlete

THERE WERE MANY CHANGES in the rules and equipment required to protect the athletes during my time.

One of the boxers in the Bengals was a victim of the limited protective equipment used by boxers. He had a good deal of boxing experience, and on this occasion, he was matched with an opponent who had formerly boxed in the Golden Gloves bouts in Chicago, also an experienced boxer.

Our man, who will be identified only as Bill, went into the ring with the usual protection worn by these boxers, consisting of a mouthpiece and a padded helmet. The bouts were well supervised, with professional referees who understood the need to stop a bout at any time when things were one-sided or when a participant was in danger of serious injury. The three rounds were of about a minute and a half each, long enough when you are in the ring.

Bill climbed into the ring, spoke with the trainer, punched one glove into the other, and then the bell rang. Bill jumped up, advanced, touched gloves with his opponent and the fight was on—but not for long! Bill took a heavy blow to the right side of his head and jaw, and everything went black. That cleared in a matter of seconds but now he had two opponents to contend with—he was seeing double. The bell rang. He sat in his corner. The trainer wiped his face with a sponge full of cool water. With his head clear, Bill finished the next two rounds.

After his shower, he was suddenly dizzy and light-headed. He reported to the trainer. The University doctor soon had him in the student infirmary for observation. He was okay in the morning and was released, feeling just a little puny. With today's more serious view of head injuries, the events following the concussion would have been managed differently. Research reveals that there may be permanent residuals of such injuries, which are manifested in later life in some individuals, by personality changes, headaches, depression, etc., even suicide.

Bill confessed to me, recently, his concern over any residual effects he might be harboring, although he has not had any problems. His anxiety relates to the fact that he suffered mild concussions on at least another half-dozen occasions, and he is aware of the recent reports of some of the residuals of such concussions.

The older players speak of the day, before my time, probably about 1947, when John "Pep" Panelli suffered a concussion during the game. He reportedly continued to play the remainder of the game but could not recall any of it the following day. That was an extremely dangerous situation. There are strict rules today governing the player's return to play after any degree of head injury. "Pep" lived a normal life and life span, despite that occasion. He was a successful businessman. He never showed any residual effects of that concussion and several more which he incurred in five years of "pro" football. He remained sharp and bright to his last days. It is fortunate that most of these players who have suffered concussion do not suffer consequences in later years. This should be a comforting thought to my friend, Bill.

Dave Duerson, another of our ex-players, is an example of a tragic outcome. His history of injuries while at Notre Dame did not reveal any head injuries. He had been one of our best players, a two-year player at safety, who proved to be a most intelligent and personable gentleman, achieving success in business and in life. After his college football career ended, he played professional football with the Chicago Bears 1983-89, the New York Giants 1990, and Arizona 1991-93. The University recognized his abilities. He was selected and served on the Board of Athletics at Notre Dame. Dave's life took a gradual downturn at about that time; this became critical in 2002. He developed personality changes; he became vindictive and abusive, and his marriage suffered. Dave recognized what was happening. He became despondent, and took his own life. He was aware of this dysfunctional development in his life and had willed his brain to science for study of residuals of this type of injury. This was one more example of what a conscientious person he was, giving his fellow men the opportunity to profit by whatever knowledge might be gained from the study of his brain. These studies confirmed the presence of residuals of head injuries that he must have suffered over the years, leading to this tragic consequence.

Extensive studies on concussion and its residuals are now being conducted. Dr. James Moriarity, current Chief of Medical Services at Notre Dame, heads up that study at the University. He has had sensors placed in the helmets in various sports as part of his study to record the forces of blows to the head that athletes suffer.

When I first started with the team, facemasks and mouth guards were not required. The dentists got their share of work on

Dr. James Moriarity, Chief of Medical Services at Notre Dame from 1985 to the present time, is doing research on head injuries.

these mouths. Most of the experienced linemen, and to an extent the others too, had big gaps in their front teeth—a pretty picture.

A few years after I started with the team, mouth guards became mandatory. Jerry Gray received the benefit of such protective equipment. He was one of our football players who had suffered several concussions. Dr. Jack Stenger, team dentist, fashioned a mouthpiece for Jerry, who had no further concussions while using the mouth guard. The dentists now provided each player with a mouth guard formed individually from molds of the player's mouth and teeth like those that boxers use.

The recent studies on the residual effects of such injuries are but part of the efforts made by ruling bodies today in hopes of preventing such injuries and outcomes. Protective equipment of various kinds has become mandatory. The helmets worn in football have been studied extensively and have undergone a number of changes in their design and construction. Because of these studies, variations on facemasks have also been devised, differing for the positions played. Certain protective pads have been designed to function best according to the demands of a particular position played by the athlete. Pads are now also required for shoulders, thighs and hips. Quarterbacks wear air-inflated vests to protect against chest injuries. Down linemen now use knee braces that offer some degree of protection against injuries to that area. Ankles are protected with various types of taping and bracing.

Changes in Treatment

IN ADDITION TO CHANGES in protective equipment, there were also changes occurring in the management of injuries. It was an early experience at Notre Dame that brought the problem of injuries to the ligaments of the knee to my attention. One of our players had suffered severe injuries to his knee—torn ligaments. I had applied a cast, which was advised at that time. On removal of the cast and early in his rehabilitation, it was evident that there remained marked laxity of the knee. The player sat on the examining table and, by alternately contracting the quadriceps muscle and then the hamstrings, with the knee at ninety degrees of flexion, he voluntarily effected subluxation, partial dislocation, of the knee joint, just as occurs with some of our tests for instability of the knee.

This knee might buckle beneath such an individual at any time that he moved with rotation and weight on it while the knee was slightly flexed. He would manage well with ordinary walking and even running activities, but he would experience this subluxation with quick starts and stops, and with cutting and rotary movements. He had completed his senior year. His athletic career was over. He returned to his home community for any further care that would be advised by the surgeon in his region. However, the surgical procedures recommended at that time were notoriously ineffective in returning the chronically unstable knee to good function, although a number of outstanding orthopaedic surgeons had developed procedures attempting to correct this deficiency. Intensive strengthening of the muscles crossing that joint would give him a functional knee for the usual activities of daily living.

It was a Swedish orthopaedic surgeon, Ivar Palmer, who made an intensive study that thoroughly defined the problem of the ligament-injured knee. He analyzed it, and made recommendations on the advisable treatment of these injured knees. His work on ligament injuries to the knee was published in a medical journal, the Acta Chirurgica Scandinavica in 1938, one not read routinely by most American physicians. As a result of his work, the treatment of these injuries changed. He advised surgical repair.

It was not until later that an American orthopaedic surgeon, Dr. Don O'Donoghue, at the University of Oklahoma, seized on this information and followed Palmer's teachings. O'Donoghue reported on a series of cases in 1950, in which he had followed the methods advocated by Palmer. Don confirmed the efficacy and practicality of the newer approach to the problem—early surgical repair. The results were better. Further reports of surgical methods and their success in the treatment of ligament injuries of the knee began to appear in our literature, and surgery became the norm.

Further improvements are occurring with time, and soon today's standards will become yesterday's. Today, this surgery is being done through the arthroscope, a method that allows more exact placement of substitute ligaments, with less surgical trauma and blood loss, less pain and faster healing. Still other new techniques are continually evolving.

One of the more common operations on the knee has been the removal of a torn cartilage, the meniscus. Today we realize the importance of preserving the meniscus. Methods to surgically repair the meniscus, when indicated, are practiced today. There are also procedures in the process of development to replace a damaged meniscus. The arthroscope has facilitated the development of these procedures.

Kneecaps that dislocate, fully or even partially, are another frequent cause of problems. Many of these can be treated without surgery. If surgery is necessary, there are multiple approaches to correct the problem. Several new surgical approaches to the problem are being developed, although the methods we had used for years seemed adequate. Shortcomings of that surgery in a fair percentage of patients have led to these changes. This area is also evolving toward a more dependable solution.

Today, there are extensive research programs in progress at

various institutions exploring the repair and replacement of defects of the surface cartilage in joints such as the knee. Other studies explore the place of hormonal growth factors in repair of tissue, the development of robotic instruments for more exact surgery, and replacement of parts of the knee.

The American Journal of Sports Medicine in 2010 published 74 articles relating to surgery for ligament injuries of the knee, and another 67 in 2011. With such research and technical changes, the orthopaedic surgeon looks to further improve his management of injuries to the ligaments of the knee. We do not yet have all the answers. Sometimes, it is necessary to resort to the trial of a procedure whose outcome is unpredictable.

Such was the case with one of my repairs of a knee that had been very severely injured. The knee was stable, but the patient did not recover the motion necessary for good function. The man was a top athlete. He was seen by a man close to the patient's home—a physician whose skills and experience were greater than mine. In this case, it was Ken Strong at the University of Rochester. He did further surgery on my patient, innovative in its way, to restore the range of motion of his knee with success. This enabled the athlete to compete at the professional level in football with the New York Giants from 1979 to 1982. Jeff Weston can certainly thank Dr. Strong for that.

Many of these top athletes who underwent surgery went on to professional careers. Surgery enabled the return of a number of these men to their sports careers. I have also seen and know what happens to these knees further on down the road. They develop post-traumatic arthritis, and almost all of them require eventual knee replacement surgery for relief of symptoms—a heavy price to pay—but almost all of them say they would do it all over again.

Even during their playing years, some of the players with

whom we worked had conditions that became painful, due to attritional, degenerative changes in the cartilage structure on the joint surface of the knee or "knee-cap," early arthritic changes. The players tolerated this degree of discomfort, some requiring mild analgesics after games but not requiring surgery.

Drugs

A NEED FOR MEDICATION resulted in an unfortunate development in one of our patients who had pain after strenuous activity due to changes in the cartilage surfacing under the kneecap. The individual was given Darvon after games, a mild analgesic, which gave him the relief he sought. Darvon was a fairly new medication at the time and was not considered to be addictive. However, the drug ameliorated pain but it also gave our player a pleasant sensation. It gave him a "fix" leading eventually to overuse and abuse of the medication. It was some time before we realized that he was getting the medication through me, as well as from Dr. Green, the University physicians, and other sources. He became addicted and required treatment. Fortunately, he was successful in breaking the habit. This problem has been reported in other schools in their athletic programs, especially those in which a bottle of such medication was available in the training room for self-administration. Such practices are no longer followed.

Today, the misuse of drugs in the general population can easily lend itself to the same problems in athletes. There are now rigid protocols for detection of drug usage in sports. Detection of such leads to disciplinary action, which may result in expulsion from the program and loss of scholarship. This problem exists at many levels of athletics.

Considerable effort is being made to discourage and prevent the use of such drugs. The pleasure-seeking drugs are one problem. The other is the desire of an athlete to gain an edge on his competitor, to find some magic drug to endow him with greater speed or strength, regardless of the consequences. Repeated instances of such drug use are being uncovered in professional athletes in many sports—athletes who seem able to perform at well above the usual levels.

Lance Armstrong is the supreme example of this in recent times. Illegal drugs used to enhance performance, undetected for some time, eventually coming to light, resulting in loss of the winner's title in his seven first-place finishes in the world's premier cycling event, the Tour de France.

These athletes set poor examples for the developing athlete who learns that such performances are the result of enhancement by illegal drugs. They too may follow that pattern. These young athletes are willing and even eager to use it themselves.

I recall an argument with a pole-vaulter at Notre Dame who insisted that steroids should be prescribed for him to give him the same chance for success at his sport that others using steroids in his sport had reported. When I refused, he intimated that he would find some other way to procure them.

Today there are compulsory routines followed to detect the use of drugs in college athletes to prevent such abuses of drugs. Meanwhile, chemists and others with knowledge of methods to produce such drugs are at work to find new drugs that will not be detected by the tests used today. It is a steady "cat and mouse" game.

Drug use is not compatible with athleticism and is not acceptable—either for the enhancement of performance, or for recreational use. In my opinion, sports should remain that athletic event which seeks to identify the best athletes performing under normal conditions. Training and work should be the answer, not drugs.

Adaptation

MOST OF THE PLAYERS did not use medications or drugs for their minor aches and pains. Some players played through their injuries. They learned to ignore the minor dysfunctional symptoms of prior injuries or some degree of residual pain with some activities. They succeeded in spite of the residuals of their injuries. This was the case with one of our guards. He had undergone surgery for the repair of torn ligaments of his knee. Postoperatively, the knee revealed some instability on certain rotary motions. He learned that he must plant that foot in internal rotation to tighten up the knee in order to keep it from buckling as he pulled out of his position as a guard on certain plays when he had to block for a runner. He trained himself to do that until it became automatic. He thereby had a functional knee. Some men developed such unconventional compensatory mechanisms to make up for such deficiencies. In this way, they were able to regain the positions they held prior to their injury. With such dedication, most of them succeeded, but not all.

One of our players was an outstanding athlete from Chicago, where he had excelled in football in many ways. At that time, a player was expected to play on defense as well as on offense. However, as a defensive player, an outside linebacker, he wasn't getting the job done as well as he seemed to have been doing at the high school level. He just was not a good tackler—and for good reason. We learned in time that, instead of tackling in the usual way, he simply threw a body block into his opponent to bring him down. Strange. Why? It turned out that he had bilateral dislocating shoulders, and he learned to avoid those dislocations that might occur when he tackled if he used his arms in the normal way. He had adapted to his medical problem. Surgical correction was performed with good result, but he did not return to football. He had gone through enough. He was not about to undertake those risks again.

Return to Play

FOLLOWING THE ACCEPTED PRINCIPLES of medical care did not necessarily guarantee a good functional result. Even with the best of surgical reconstructions or repairs of a knee, for example, a truly objective evaluation of the result would find it short of perfection. Some of these knees were acceptable for certain activities, such as that of a "down" lineman; but that knee might not be acceptable in a running back. The ability to start and stop quickly, to twist and dart one way and another, to turn on the speed and to carry a load of men on one's back required a good solid knee that had undergone the highest levels of rehabilitation, strengthening, and performance of functional activities to a degree that would return the man to competition. One could not guarantee that the end-result would allow that.

Sometimes a player might be given a trial of function, a chance to participate, and there were times when the functional performance of that knee was adequate. Such was the case with John Scully, our first-string center in 1979 and 1980. His anterior cruciate ligament had been torn, but the joint capsule and medial ligaments were still holding well. He played with a brace on his somewhat unstable knee; but if that knee had been that of a running back and was not stable, not adequate, that knee would be reinjured very quickly.

As a result of their sports injuries, some athletes were unable to resume their sport at the elite level at which they had played earlier. When unable to participate, or if such would further endanger the player, his participation was terminated. Painful as it was, there were those who were thankful years later for stopping them at that point, before they suffered a more disabling condition.

At times, such players were taken off the roster and given a job with the team, possibly as an assistant coach. The scholarships would continue, like those of other athletes who were dismissed from the team because of injuries. This satisfied the desire of the players to remain with the activities of the team.

Dennis Gutowski was one of these. He appeared initially to have a great career ahead of him. He was highly regarded by the coaches. Here was a young man of unusual abilities as a halfback and defensive back. He was in the starting lineup for the game with Northwestern early in the season one year. In the first series of plays, in which he participated, he suffered one of the more severe injuries to the ligaments of the knee. Surgical repair was necessary. The result was considered to be a good one, but his knee was not perfect. There was slight residual instability. After his rehabilitation, he was given a trial of function, but his abilities on his return to his position as a halfback were not on a par with his previous performance.

He tried hard, but the knee was not good enough for running, cutting, and dodging tackles at bad angles, using the knee in strained positions, etc. He suffered several episodes of sprains and giving way of that knee during these trials of function before he agreed that he could not function as a halfback. Try as he would, he was not going to recover his elusive, as well as powerful, performances. He agreed that he was no longer up to the job.

At the end of the season, we had a heart-to-heart talk. He realized that he was unlikely to regain his previous form and would not be playing the games he had looked forward to. There was also the possibility that further injury could result in a lasting and more severe disability to him. It was heart breaking, but I felt I had to disqualify him; after due consideration, he agreed to give up football.

It was a number of years later that he sent me a letter, thanking me for that frank discussion. Dennis Gutowski gave me one of those opportunities to be the "complete physician" back in 1972. A letter he sent me, years after I had disqualified him for football, is that of a grateful patient, despite the unfavorable outcome in his case. My mentoring at that crucial stage of his life had been done with empathy and understanding, and with concern for his emotional well-being.

In these later years, he valued the fact that the knee was good enough to play ball with his children, an activity which he realized he might have missed had the knee been again or more seriously injured. Dennis remains a grateful patient despite the fact that I disqualified him for football at Notre Dame following his injury.

One of my most disheartening duties came when I found it necessary to disqualify any athlete who had suffered a serious injury—possibly one which had required surgery—that had required laborious rehabilitation of the injured part but, in the end, with the man still not capable of competing at his previous level. Such a man would have been reinjured, probably many times, if allowed to return to the type of competition in which these football players engage. And yet, it was many of these very athletes who were still eager to play. Our obligation was first to our patient, to do and advise what was best for him.

Most physicians are all too human. They are brought to

Dennis Gutowski suffered an injury to his knee, the "terrible triad" tearing the anterior cruciate and medial ligaments and medial meniscus of the knee. Residual laxity after surgery and rehabilitation ended his football career.

their station, to begin with, by the desire to occupy a helpful and responsible position in the health-related affairs of society. They study and train arduously, hoping to do their job and do it well. Each of us looks forward to gaining the patient's well-being because of these efforts. Good results are gratifying in themselves. Further gratification is found in the expression of the patient who perceives the value of a physician's work, as expressed in their eyes and faces, or in other ways. We may sympathize and empathize with our student-athlete patients, but our primary consideration remains his well-being. This means the rendering of unpopular decisions when necessary.

Occasionally gratitude appears years later, as demonstrated in the letter from Dennie Gutowski, grateful after years, whereas he first resented me for moving to disqualify him for football because the condition of his knee would have led to repeated and disabling injury. It may take years to develop the appreciation of that act. In most cases, we feel better compensated in knowing that a patient is grateful, rather than in the financial compensation.

Other players demonstrated their satisfaction in other ways. Walt Patulski gave me his hard-earned trophy as the outstanding player in the game with the University of Miami in 1971. This was after his dislocated shoulder had undergone surgical correction, returning him to function impressively thereafter.

Most of the injured took their treatment for granted, realizing that the school had arranged for their care to be conducted by capable hands. They accepted it as their due, as they were entitled to do—a reasonable assumption. Some recognized the special training and efforts on our part in bringing them back to playing condition. Some made special effort to acknowledge this. Three of these were linemen, ends, who returned to highly competitive activity, regaining their positions as first-string players at Notre Dame, and continuing into the professional ranks.

Each of these men made a special effort near the end of their senior year to see me personally, to thank me for the work I had done on them, before they left ND. One of these was Walt Patulski who went on to play at Buffalo, 1972-75, and St. Louis 1977; I repaired a recurring dislocation of the shoulder on him. Another was Alan Page, on whom I did the same surgery. He played at Minnesota, 1967-78, and Chicago 1978-81. The third was Mark Bavarro, who also underwent repair of a dislocating shoulder. He played with the New York Giants 1985-90, Cleveland 1992, and Philadelphia 1993-94.

Was there something special in the psyche of these men? Was there something that made them more appreciative or demonstrative than others, and yet made them so tough as to be of the best of them? Or was it just a coincidence? Probably the latter, but I was glad to see this aspect of these men who had proven themselves men in every aspect of manhood, and who played with near savage intensity when necessary, and yet men who in their daily lives continued to maintain a proper appreciation for the help given them by others in attaining their goals.

Others showed it in ways that are more social. Bill "Red"

Alan Page played 14 years professionally, 1967-81.   Mark Bavarro played 9 years professionally, 1985-94.

Mack was one of those. He always insisted that we have a drink together when I saw him at the annual meeting of the Monogram Club at Notre Dame. He was a good friend, all heart, on the field and off.

When the results of treatment are not as good as the player expected, there is great disappointment—especially when surgery has been necessary. There is then a great sense of disappointment by the player and the physician. I experienced that in the care of one of our players who suffered the more unusual type of

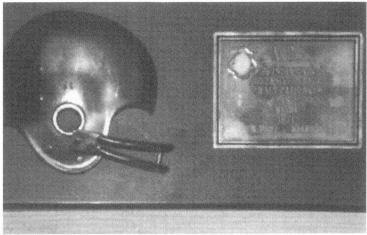

Walter Patulski played 5 years professionally, 1972-77. He received the award pictured here honoring him as the outstanding player in the game with Miami in 1971. Walter gave me this trophy in appreciation of the successful surgery that enabled him to continue his career in football.

ligament injury to his knee for which I did surgical repair. He had torn the posterior cruciate ligament and the medial ligaments and capsule including the posteromedial corner of the knee. Access to the posterior aspect of the knee is difficult and requires special caution because of the nerve and vascular structures bridging the area. The repair was done but the outcome of such repairs of the cruciate ligament may remain questionable. In this case, there was residual instability, enough to be of concern to anyone hopeful of returning to contact sports. At times, the condition can be corrected or at least improved upon; and sometimes there will be an inferior result to the disappointment of all concerned.

Critical Situations

IN LOOKING AFTER THESE MEN, some critical situations did arise. Despite all precautions, unexpected and unusual injuries and conditions did arise. They were usually witnessed by someone from the medical team at the site and received prompt attention; however, there may be an occasional one that escaped detection.

There was the occasion when the team played in Philadelphia. I was not there. Dr. George Green, the team physician and surgeon, had gone with the team. The game was the usual hard-hitting, tough-going game. After the game, the fellows cleaned up, dressed, and returned to the hotel where they were to stay. The team went to dinner after the game but Dick Szymanski did not appear. His teammates reported to the trainer and Dr. Green that the player did not feel well and was having some abdominal discomfort, so he preferred to stay in bed in his room. George went up to see him, and in a short time had Szymanski hospitalized and in surgery for a laceration of the spleen. Dick had taken a heavy blow to the abdominal region, lacerating the spleen, a highly vascular organ. There was steady, slow bleeding into the abdomen from this injury, not obvious externally. This could well have been fatal within a short time. The spleen was removed. Dick lived to play again.

During my time, we have been fortunate at Notre Dame to have had very few of those extremely serious and near fatal injuries to our players, such as fatal head injuries or paralyzing neck injuries, either during the practices or the football games, or in other sports. If I were superstitious about such things, I would want to knock on wood as I write this. Of course, I am not superstitious but I will knock on wood anyway. Why tempt fate?

The only fatality associated with sports in our group of athletes, with which I am familiar, occurred the year before I joined the program. Ray Espenan was conducting a class on the use of the trampoline while practice teaching at Central High School in South Bend. (Notre Dame had a school of physical education in those days.) Ray was an end on the football team, a well-coordinated athlete. He was demonstrating a flip-flop maneuver to his class when he unfortunately missed the trampoline. He came down on his head and neck. He suffered a high cervical fracture-dislocation and was immediately paralyzed from the neck down.

He received good care, but there really is no treatment that can alter that paralysis—and this is true even today. The spinal cord had been injured so close to the brain that he expired within a few days—a terrible misfortune, a rare injury, one that may occur in many sports. This is one of the worst possible injuries that I can imagine, with complete loss of sensation and loss of the ability to move any part of the body below the area innervated by that segment of the spinal cord that has been injured. Ray had played a lot of tough football without serious injury, and it was certainly a sorry day, a great misfortune, to have this trampoline episode (so often judged as child's play) as the cause of this fatal experience in a sports event. The trampoline is a dangerous piece of equipment.

A near fatality occurred during two-a-day practices in 1968 when Joe Freebery suddenly collapsed, while standing on the sidelines, just after he had come out after some plays. He was pulseless and had stopped breathing. Dr. George Colip was the University physician on the field at the time. He administered

CPR and revived the player promptly. Extensive medical workup and studies following this event did not reveal the exact cause of this collapse. Was it heat-related? Could be. It was a hot day. Was it cardiac arrest from some blow to the chest? He did not recall any. No, it wasn't a head injury. The player was discouraged from returning to play thereafter. It was not safe. He did not lose his scholarship. Notre Dame continues the athletic scholarships in these cases of injury that prevents the player's return to his sport.

It was also a good example of why there was always a physician on the field during contact workouts. Fortunately, such instances are rare. Nevertheless, they do occur when least expected. The medical team must be prepared to act in such emergencies. We did practice such scenarios each fall. The maneuvers in moving a spinal-injured patient applied equally to other situations where moving the patient and transporting him required special care.

Injuries on the Field

SOMETIMES IT IS POSSIBLE and even best that an injury is managed right on the field at the time of injury. Willie Townsend suffered a dislocation of the head of the radius of his elbow in practice one day. It was simple to manipulate and reduce then and there when he willed himself to relax the protective muscle spasm that initially accompanies that injury.

The trick in these situations is to get to the patient before the muscle spasm becomes "fixed" and persuade the player to allow his muscles to relax, to "go loose" to enable the parts to be easily replaced to their normal location.

One of our basketball players, Ray Martin, suffered a fracture-dislocation of an ankle in a game with Indiana at Notre Dame. I

Ray Martin suffered a fracture-dislocation of his ankle shortening his playing career.

was there immediately since I also covered basketball and hockey games at that time. Martin lay in pain on the floor. He had suffered a severe twisting injury to the ankle as he came down on the side of his foot from a jump under the basket. He lay on the floor with his ankle in the typical position of that injury, a deformity with the foot turned sideways and at a right angle to the leg. Again, out on the floor, while supporting the foot, I quietly and quickly explained the need to consciously relax the muscles about the foot and ankle, which Ray did, so that I easily and with very little pain to him reduced the dislocation. I manipulated the ankle while maintaining gentle traction and had it slip back into place, to his great relief. The leg was splinted and surgery was performed the next day, accurately reducing the ankle joint, fixing the fibula with plate and screws. His subsequent course was good, but his recovery took a lot of time and therapy. Although it was good enough to return to play sports, he had lost enough functional ability of that part that he ultimately stopped playing, and later turned to coaching instead.

Finger joints were frequently dislocated. Most of them reduced easily, even without an anesthetic. One of the more troublesome ones is the thumb joint when dislocated at the junction of the thumb with the hand. It usually reduces easily with a little tricky traction and manipulation. However, if it doesn't reduce, you are likely dealing with the type in which the head of the thumb metacarpal has perforated the capsule and is caught there, the intervening capsule obstructing the reduction. Surgery is usually necessary in these cases.

George Kunz suffered this type of injury in practice one day. I met him as he came off the field. The trainers had tried unsuccessfully to reduce the dislocated thumb. We went to the hospital where I did a sterile prep on him under nerve block anesthesia. The skin was incised and I came down on this strong capsule drawn tightly about the metacarpal head, which had slipped through a small buttonhole in the capsule. Traction now only caused the capsule to fit more tightly about the metacarpal, just as a Japanese "finger trap" tightens around one's finger holding it more tightly as traction is applied. It was necessary to further cut the capsule so that traction now pulled the finger into normal position. The capsule and wound were closed and a cast was applied. He played with a cast on his hand and thumb for several weeks thereafter until I was sure that stability of the joint would be maintained. This healed uneventfully.

Other types of injury may require the care of other disciplines, sometimes as emergencies, and sometimes away from home. The trainers at Clemson were very cooperative on an occasion there when one of our players suffered an injury to the cornea of his eye. Their ophthalmologist was called out of the stands to give us advice on management of that injury. Such cooperation exists between medical groups, and I was grateful for it.

Yes, when they are needed, the medical team is a vital part of the athletic team, and it is now recognized that their services should be available on the spot, and that the medical team be capable of managing the various conditions that may present themselves. They must be prepared when "their number is

The medical team in 1984 from left to right: Dr. Robert Thompson, Medical Director and Team Doctor; Gene Paszkiet, Head Trainer; Dr. George Green, Surgeon and Team Doctor; Dr. Les Bodnar, Orthopaedic Surgeon and Team Doctor.

called" like any other member of the team. Those on the sideline, especially the medical staff, must maintain their composure while managing the emergency. Maintaining such a mental state under duress is no different from that which the seasoned ballplayer does at critical times. Some of them are so well trained that they actually seem to perform best when under pressure. This has been well demonstrated by various players who find themselves in the limelight in a play that is particularly important to the team. At various times, quarterbacks, receivers, kickers, and centers are especially likely to have every eye in the stadium focused on them. That is not the time for the timid, or for stage fright. A good part of their success has to be attributed to their mastery of their emotions and the ability to concentrate on their job in tense situations.

Unusual Circumstances

OVER THE YEARS, many of the problems we dealt with were somewhat routine, but some injuries did occur under unusual circumstances.

I recall one injury that occurred on "Media Day." A media photographer wanted to shoot a picture of a dramatic tackle being made. A runner was sent through his paces and was fiercely tackled by one of his teammates. This was exactly the action the photographer wanted. However, the runner did not get up after the tackle. Sadly, we learned that his knee had been injured. Surgery was done in the next few days for a torn and displaced cartilage, a "locked" knee. That player returned to the team in due time and fulfilled the obligations of his scholarship. A high price in human suffering was paid for that photo.

In cases of severe injury, we could hospitalize patients for treatment or observation or admit them to the student infirmary when this occurred at home. However, the situation could be more complicated on the road. Visiting teams encountered the same problem at Notre Dame home games.

A Northwestern University player suffered a severe injury on one of the occasions when we played Northwestern University in South Bend. At one point in the game, they elected to punt the ball. One of the Northwestern players blocked our rushing lineman into the kicker's leg just as the kicker's leg sailed through the kicking motion. The kicker incurred a compound fracture of the tibia, resulting in the large bone below the knee protruding through the skin. This required prompt surgery. Immediate wound care was given and the patient was hospitalized. Dr. Howard Sweeney, the orthopaedic surgeon who traveled with the Northwestern team assisted me in the surgery on his player.

A year later, at Northwestern, Howard brought the man over to see me. The player had graduated and was no longer in school. He had recovered completely from his injury and thanked me for my work. I was glad to see the good result. Most gratifying.

A visiting team member incurred another major injury during my first season when our Notre Dame player made a hard tackle on an Indiana University player during a punt return. With his leg in the fully extended position and his foot on the ground at the moment of impact, our man tackled him at thigh level, fracturing the femur—the large bone of the thigh—at its middle third. The Indiana player was in severe pain with that injury. The player was sedated on the field. I carefully and with light traction straightened the leg. A Thomas splint was applied. The ambulance, which was always stationed just outside of the stadium, was brought onto the field, and the patient was stabilized. Soon after the game, he was flown back to Bloomington.

On another occasion, a Navy player suffered a serious injury. He lay on our field, in pain, after the play, which had seemed like a routine tackle at knee level. His foot was planted at the moment of the injury. The momentum of his body carried him in one direction as he was tackled from the other direction. The knee buckled awkwardly. I was at his side immediately since this had occurred very close to our side of the field. "Red" Romer, the Navy trainer, was also there quickly, as was their doctor, Joe Godfrey. I was the first one to reach him. His knee was almost completely dislocated. I was able to have the player relax his muscles, and with gentle traction, I reduced the knee on the field with very little pain to him. Dislocations usually reduce easily if done properly before muscle spasm sets in. The man was hospitalized at St. Joseph Medical Center. An arteriogram was done with normal findings, no tearing of the vital vascular structures of the knee, and nerve functions were intact. He was observed overnight for any complication that might occur, such as a tear of the lining membrane of an artery, which can make a delayed appearance. His condition remained good and the next day he was flown back to Annapolis for definitive surgery by Dr. Godfrey.

Some of the injuries that have been described are typical of what may occur in practice sessions or in games, as well as in recreational activities. The injuries varied considerably in the degree to which they were serious—some requiring surgery, some requiring long-term care and rehabilitation, and some terminating the athlete's playing days. Fortunately, such injuries as those to the neck resulting in fractures and paralysis, severe concussions, and compound fractures and dislocations of major bones and joints are rare. Injuries to the nose, jaws, and teeth occur frequently. Other injuries to the back, abdominal organs, and the vital organs of the chest are all rare occurrences. In practically all of these situations, it is enough that the condition is promptly recognized for what it is. Treatment may be urgent. In some cases, it may be delayed without danger to the patient. Decisions must be made to treat them promptly, or to transfer them to a hospital or training room for better control of the situation if it so demands. Consultations with other specialists may be required for certain cases. The medical team is familiar with these situations and has a plan of action for these injuries. Training of ancillary personnel and advance provision of equipment necessary for such emergencies—including provisions for transportation, arrangements for hospital facilities if needed, and a host of other preparations for the above—are but part of the responsibilities of the medical team.

The Coaches

IN DEALING WITH the medical problems and injuries of all players, it was important to keep the coaches, and especially the head coach, informed of the health status of the athletes. The coaches were truly concerned, not only for the sake of their plans for these players, but mainly because of their personal interest in the individual. In recruiting, it had been promised that the person would be well cared for, and there was often personal involvement by coaches who had visited with the athletes' families during the recruiting period. The degree of this involvement varied from one coach to another. The coaches differed in their attitudes during my thirty-five years. Early, they were defensive about medical decisions; later, they realized we were working toward the same goals, to restore and maintain the player's well-being, for the good of the team and all other concerned interests.

With some coaches, their faith in us was just a matter of time and the result of witnessing our results. With us, it was a matter that required patience until that faith developed. The questions always arose: Can we trust this doctor's advice and decisions? The answer was in the sum of our professionalism, our training and ability, and that deciding factor—the safe return of the player to action—which marked one as being capable and cooperative, the man for the job. Communication was an important factor in the doctor-patient-coach relationship. Such communication was not always an acceptable and reciprocal one. We had to establish our credibility with each new coach. That's just how it was.

Coach Frank Leahy
1941-1943, 1946-1953

FRANK LEAHY, a name synonymous with football at the time, was the head coach at Notre Dame in 1949. He had come to "Our Lady's School" in the fall of 1941 from Boston College, where he had a record of twenty wins and two losses. Coach Leahy had been called on to restore the great days of Notre Dame Football, and both the coach and the administration were confident of his ability to succeed. He served in the service of the U.S. Navy, 1943-46, after which time he returned to continue his winning program at Notre Dame.

Leahy was an intense man, a good Catholic, devoted to his wife and family, but above all, a man obsessed by football, especially of the winning kind. He lost no time in establishing his coaching staff and restructuring the program to restore the school to its position of glory. Leahy's success in eleven years as head football coach at Notre Dame would include eighty-seven wins, eleven losses, nine ties, and four National Championships (1943, 1946, 1947, and 1949). The coach earned a revered spot in Notre Dame history that placed him next to Knute Rockne, who occupied the position of honor on the mantel alone for so many years.

The coach was his own man. He held himself aloof. His demeanor did not invite socialization. He was a hard taskmaster, hard on himself as well as on his coaches and players. It was not unusual in practice sessions to have him work his players to near exhaustion, only to have them finish the practice with another lap or two around the field. The players dragged themselves off the field, muttering to themselves, but once they finished football at

Head Coach Frank Leahy, "The Master"

Notre Dame, most of them referred to him respectfully, in fact almost affectionately as "The Master."

He was also a master psychologist, capable of getting the best out of a man in various ways, not always kindly. I recall one game, I believe it was with USC, when he pulled one of our most reputable linemen, Bob Toneff, out of the game. He obviously was not pleased with Toneff's play. USC had successfully run several plays through him. The coach sat Toneff on the bench near him. He ignored Toneff for a number of plays. Then he half-turned to the player and politely asked him if his parents were at the game. Toneff assured him they were. Frank spoke in a kindly tone. "It's too bad they came all this way to see you play." There was a short silence for a play or two. "They must be very ashamed of the way you are letting your opponents walk over you." Again, a short period of silence. "You must not tell them that you really tried to do your best because I know you are not trying hard enough."

Toneff sat there dumbfounded and angered. A few minutes later, Leahy sent him back into the game. On the next play, Toneff broke through the line and blocked the USC kick, giving ND the ball, a golden opportunity, with good position on the field. It wasn't long before we scored. Toneff came off the field looking the coach straight in the eye as he walked off.

Coach Leahy was indeed "The Master." His manner was reserved, thoughtful, it seemed, and certainly distant. He carried himself with dignity, although his back was slightly rounded, and yet he presented the picture of a man going purposefully about his work, not one about to have his attention diverted by mundane interests. This was all part of a wall he had built about himself, preserving his privacy and whatever other thoughts or activities permeated his shell.

He typically spoke in a quiet, somewhat formal, and gentlemanly tone. And he wanted his "boys," his "lads," to recognize themselves as "gentlemen." He reminded them often of their good fortune to be part of the program at "Our Lady's School," and that he wished them to represent her well—and they did, most of the time. They fought hard for the Glory of Notre Dame. He developed their work ethic, their confidence in their ability to win, and the teamwork that brought them success. They were comrades in this, having suffered mutually under "the Master." This incorporated them into the fabric of the Notre Dame family.

That was not the nature of the coach's relationship with the medical team. Here he maintained what could be regarded as an authoritarian presence, which was not to be subjected to unpleasant nor unwelcome decisions. Until this time, he had a few doctors whom he felt he could trust and with whom he could communicate. He counted on favorable decisions from them on returning injured players to play if there was no question on the severity of that man's condition. I am tempted to use the word manipulate here in reference to the manner in which such consultations were sometimes conducted with physicians who were eager to seek his favor. Such actions by some coaches were not unusual in those days.

I had very little direct contact with Coach Leahy. There were few occasions when it would have been necessary. The trainer, Dr. Green, and Dr. Egan dealt directly with the coach, keeping him informed of whatever problems arose. I must have been a cipher in his estimation, a man without a record, without a following, with only a few people to recommend me. I had to prove that I was the man for the job. I learned in time that Dr. Green had been brought in as team physician shortly after I started with the program to appease Leahy who wanted an older, more experienced man with whom he had already established relationships and in whom he had confidence to look after his players.

The trainers were under his control. They knew their job as one to get the player well enough to play. They did not entertain any ideas of holding a man out for rehabilitation any longer than the coach saw fit. They saw themselves working for Coach Leahy, rather than for the players or the University. Moreover, he did not see the doctors as part of the team, intimately concerned with the welfare of the players. In fact, his attitude was contrary to that position.

I was informed at one time that Coach Leahy had stood before the assembled athletes advising them to "stay away from the doctors," that they were more interested in seeing that Michigan and Illinois won, than they were in Notre Dame. (Dr. Denham graduated from Michigan, and I from Illinois.) It was at times like this that I felt that we were regarded as the enemy rather than an integral part of the team.

In most cases, it was just a matter of time before we had satisfied the coaches that we knew what we were doing and that we were on their side, despite our higher allegiance to our patients, for the good of all concerned.

Leahy's lack of compliance in the care of the injured athlete was but another rut, which had now developed in Leahy's road to greatness. His road was already rough, not the smooth road expected by the victor. On the contrary, his successes had led to a sense of dominance whereby he seemed to see his role at the University to be above other considerations. There was the sense that he saw football as his show. He was not to be harassed by University rules and regulations.

Under Coach Leahy, Notre Dame had regained its days of

glory. Winning football was again the standard fare. The alumni overall were pleased with this. They did not mention or compare the school's academic ranking with others of these higher centers of education. There was no one more aware of this deficiency than the good fathers of the Congregation of Holy Cross. It was their school. Their pride dictated that Notre Dame give their students as good and as sound an education as possible. The Congregation of Holy Cross demanded it of themselves that Notre Dame be considered among the best of schools, and not only in football. Academic standards were to be elevated.

The priests of the Congregation of Holy Cross, the religious

Reverend Edmund P. Joyce C.S.C. (on left) and Reverend Theodore M. Hesburgh C.S.C.

order that operated the University, now began to move toward their goal, long envisioned, which would make the school one of the foremost in the nation, educating and shaping the future of their young students.

The administration would seek to emphasize academics above athletics and to continue with an athletic program that was representative of the better qualities of their young men. There were some undesirable aspects of sports, which had once tainted Notre Dame's reputation. In its early days, its heralded athletes observed the rules governing student conduct only superficially, whereas other students were tightly held to them. There was some laxity in observation of the rules by which the University and its students were to abide, from which the athletes assumed that they had a special dispensation. The legendary George Gipp was a case in point, with the "Gipper" playing for money on pro teams at times, under an assumed name at still other times, failing to attend classes regularly, and famous for his gambling, pool playing, and for his flouting of many other rules, while enrolled at Notre Dame. But he could play football! He proved himself to be a Notre Dame man on the gridiron. Fortunately, such wayward activities by the athletes had subsided by the time of the post-war period of which I write, leaving only a few such rough spots to be ironed out amongst the athletes. There were always those seeking special privileges.

The abuses mentioned had drawn the attention of the Rev. John J. Cavanaugh, C.S.C., President of the University of Notre Dame in the years 1946 to 1952. His main concern was the untoward influence of athletics on the academic aspects of higher education. He and Father Hesburgh saw the emphasis on sports to be greater than on academics, creating a monster that was at odds with the stated goals of the University. Although they too were proud of Notre Dame's standing as a powerhouse in football, they did not wish to allow it to overshadow the real mission of the school, the education of young men, preparing them for their role in real life. These thoughts formed a cloud hovering over the Golden Dome and "Our Lady" at Notre Dame. The Rev. Father Theodore Hesburgh, C.S.C. and Father John Cavanaugh had agonized over these problems for some time. Father Ted had been appointed Vice-President of the University in 1949. With the end of Father Cavanaugh's presidency in 1952, Father Hesburgh became President of the University of Notre Dame. He was determined to bring Notre Dame into the circle of the more academic universities. The Rev. Edmond P. Joyce, C.S.C. would join him in initiating the changes that were to follow at Notre Dame.

The more demanding standards at the school limited the pool of eligible players. As the level of coaching and the distribution of talent became more equal throughout this top tier of schools, the competition also became more equal. Notre Dame found that it had to work harder to get their share of the best players who could also qualify academically. Competition for these athletes was tougher. Nevertheless, the good fathers had made their decision.

There was complete agreement among them. Academic excellence became the prime interest of the good fathers at Notre Dame; it did not however, replace the interest in the Notre Dame sports programs. The school would be one that excelled among the other institutions of higher learning. Higher educational standards would be established. A more notable faculty was to be assembled. A faculty with higher academic rankings would elevate the quality of the research and teaching at the University. "Chairs" in various spheres of learning would be endowed, and a library would be developed complementing the academic prestige which was the goal of Fathers Cavanaugh and Hesburgh. The notorious sport of football was to be de-emphasized. And athletes, including football players, were expected to meet these academic standards. Classroom attendance was required; no corners were to be cut; grades had to be earned; no snap courses. Athletes would be subjected to the same discipline by which all students were expected to abide. If an athlete needed help to succeed in class, tutors and mentors were at hand for those willing to try harder, but nothing more.

Finding talented players capable of meeting Notre Dame's heightened academic requirements became a problem. Notre Dame continued to recruit its share of select players, but no longer with unfailing success.

Other changes were mandated by the NCAA at about this time, further challenging Coach Leahy's dominion. It was ruled that there be certain limitations to the number of players on scholarship, as well as the number of players on the varsity roster.

The move in that direction—greater emphasis on academics coupled with the diminished emphasis on football, as well as the changes mandated by the NCAA—had already started when Terry Brennan, vaunted Notre Dame football player of the years 1945 to 1949, was brought in as coach of the freshman team in 1953. Terry was well known to all associated with Notre Dame as well as by those who followed the fortunes of the school, especially because of its football fame. Terry's share in that fame was firmly established in the annals of Notre Dame football when he returned the opening kickoff against Army in 1947, during an era in which Army football ruled the nation's gridirons and Notre Dame was threatening it. Notre Dame won that game, 27-7.

Terry had the sense of a kindly understanding with Father Hesburgh. Both Terry and his wife, Kel, saw Father Ted as one who had a special interest in Terry—a friend, highly supportive of Terry's position at Notre Dame. It seemed to them that Father

Hesburgh saw Terry as an outstanding young man, a graduate of ND with a degree in philosophy, a man who had further equipped himself for the future with a law degree earned at De Paul University while coaching at Mount Carmel High School in Chicago from 1949 to 1953.

Here was a squeaky-clean Notre Dame man, married to Mary Louise Kelly, a St. Mary's girl, both more Irish than St. Patrick himself. With Terry's academic and sports credentials, he would fit well into the future that was envisioned for him. Terry was appointed coach of the Freshman Team. At that time freshmen could not play football with the varsity team. Terry knew how to work with these young men. His teams won the all Chicago High School Football Championships in 1950, '51, and '52.

At this point Notre Dame had made its decisions, placing further limitations on the football program: fewer scholarships, restriction of funds, and strict observance of the rules and limitations as required by the NCAA. These were ground-shaking changes at Notre Dame; they would alter the beauty of the Irish landscape. The reign of Coach Leahy was to be shaken.

NATIONAL CHAMPIONS
1945, 1946, 1947, and 1949

When Leahy, one of the icons of football and a man who seemed secure in his role, was informed of the changes that would occur—in effect diminishing his football program—he rebelled. Frank Leahy had brought fame back to the Notre Dame Football Program. His teams hold the legendary record of 39 consecutive games without a loss. He developed six undefeated teams and directed its teams to four National Championships in football. But now, the football program was to be of less importance in the life of Notre Dame.

These changes did not fit well with Leahy. Theretofore he had conducted his program as his personal domain within the University. This was no longer to be the case. Since he would not tolerate the coming changes, Coach Leahy was replaced by the fledgling Terry Brennan, who was appointed Head Football Coach in 1955. Coach Leahy's record of 87 wins, 11 losses, and 9 ties over the course of his eleven years at Notre Dame remains unbeaten in Notre Dame history.

Coach Terry Brennan
1954-1958

HERE WAS A MAN, as capable a football coach as they come at 26, his age when he became head coach. In his career as a player at Notre Dame, as a two-way starter for four years (1954-1958) he was the leading scorer on the team. He was the leading pass receiver in 1946 and 1947, two of the years in which the teams were National Champions. His coaching record at Mt. Carmel High School in Chicago testified to his ability to compete with the best. He was well versed in football. He was young, intelligent, capable, and articulate. Despite the recent limitations imposed on the program at Notre Dame, he was willing to fight the odds. He was, however, initially naive to the expectations of the alumni and their later supplications and demands, which even the Notre Dame hierarchy had underestimated.

It was into this world of football that Terry entered, now as a coach. Under him, those tough young Catholics and others were welcomed: Italians, Irish, Poles, Lithuanians, and the others all had a chance to play at "their school" for Terry. However, with the higher admission standards, recruiting became more difficult and limited. Many fine athletes were turned away, unable to meet these requirements.

The incoming freshmen had proven their abilities in high school and were among the elite of high school athletes. They had achieved to the highest levels possible for developing players, but there was still need for smart coaching to bring these youngsters, many still only eighteen years old, to the performance levels of their older, more mature, more advanced, and more experienced players. They had yet to learn the finer points of the game. At that time, it was still the presumption that Notre Dame had access to the "cream of the crop" of players to be recruited each year, especially those coming from Catholic schools. It was said that the coaches and priests at their schools saw to it that the best of the lot, those athletes showing great promise, would find their way to ND.

There were enough good players who found their way to the school to field a good football team; however, success did not necessarily follow them. Terry's first two years were eminently successful; but when winning tapered off after that, the alumni rose up in arms. Various reasons have been suggested for this. Some said that Terry was too young and inexperienced, that he was not as demanding of his players as he could have been, that team discipline was poor, and so on. If these were true, there were also the usual factors in football working against Coach Brennan. Losing players in one way or another, including academics and injuries, also worked against success for the team. One of these was the loss of one of Coach Brennan's most outstanding players.

Ray Lemek, right tackle and Captain of the team in 1955, had "blown out" his knee early in the fall. This knee required surgical repair. In surgery it was found that the entire capsule of the knee medially and postero-medially, and the anterior cruciate ligament were torn and avulsed from the tibia. I had advised surgical repair. This was our first major injury under Terry. His mind followed the usual pattern. He did not know me or my work as yet. Terry checked with Dr. Jim Callahan in Chicago. Dr. Callahan was an older and highly respected orthopaedic surgeon, who had looked

Ray Lemek, right tackle and Captain of the team in 1955.

after many athletes, including Notre Dame men. He apparently had learned of me when I was a panelist on knee injuries at a sports medical symposium in Chicago. He gave his approval, giving me carte blanche to proceed with the repair.

The surgery went well, although the procedure of repairing the cruciate ligament itself was an exercise in futility. It was repaired but time has proven that the ligament simply did not heal. It did not have an adequate blood supply to do so, and such repair did not re-establish the normal stability of the knee. With anterior advancement of the capsule as it was repaired, a method advised by Dr. James Nichlas of New York at that time, some stability was added to the knee. The knee was then fairly stable and, although not normal, he did well.

Ray was able to make an appearance on the playing field by the end of the home season. Ray had played enough before his injury so that he needed just a little time in at least one more quarter of actual play to get his letter for that year, even though he was captain of the team. He was well along in his rehabilitation by then, so it was arranged with Terry that Ray would be allowed to return to the field for one play that fall. His return was dramatic. Terry put Ray in as a "lonesome end" for the last play of the home season, a position where no one would touch him. There were wild cheers from the crowd and his fellow players as Ray went in for that last minute or so. He thereby qualified for his monogram letter. He had earned one for every one of his three years of football at Notre Dame. He played the next year, earning his fourth letter. Ray then went on into the pro ranks. He played with Washington in 1957-61, and Pittsburgh in 1961-65. He remained a capable first-string player, even with the slight deficiency in knee stability.

Terry and I became good friends over the years, but at the time of decision making in Ray's case, Terry was like other coaches.

He checked me out with Dr. Callahan. This was another case of needing to prove oneself capable for the job at Notre Dame.

During those years when I was looking after the teams, the players seemed resigned to their fate, come what may. The threats of injury, surgery, and even the possibility of a career-ending condition were accepted as one of the possible outcomes of participation in football. If injured, they worked hard to overcome that injury, dedicated to their recovery and rehabilitation. They did whatever it took to return to prime form. I can still see them in the weight and training rooms, grunting, groaning, and sweating with the effort of their workouts—neck veins distended, faces flushed and red with their efforts, struggling against free weights or Nautilus equipment as they labored—paying the price to return to play. They pushed themselves through drills to restore flexibility, agility, quickness, and the particular skills required in their positions. In addition, they underwent strengthening and mobilizing programs, in the arduous process of their rehabilitation.

Despite the limitations now imposed on the football program by the NCAA as well as the school, Terry and the new coaches hoped to continue the winning traditions of Notre Dame football. Their record was 9-1-0 in 1954 and 8-2-0 in 1955, but in 1956, it fell to 2-8. Somewhere along the line and in the world of football, things were changing.

Because of Notre Dame's higher academic requirements, some of the finest players went to other schools; consequently, the won-lost records at ND suffered. This became a negative factor in recruiting. Notre Dame continued to have a goodly number of fine athletes join Terry's teams. There were still the Paul Hornungs, the "Red" Macks, the Ray Lemeks, and other athletes showing great promise, who found their way to Our Lady's School, but the situation had changed. Many of these good Catholic players now went to other schools. The talent available had to be combined with good coaching to produce winners. Now it was found that capable coaching had also become more widely distributed. As a result, any advantage Notre Dame may have had in coaching and in the number of good players they attracted was relatively diminished. Notre Dame also came to realize that there was a lot of very superior talent to be found among the African-American athletes. In 1953, the first of these black athletes to join the football team were Wayne Edmonds, a future pro-player, and Gene Washington.

Since Notre Dame had decided to de-emphasize football, it was of little wonder that the program became less successful. However, the administration had decided that this was acceptable as long as we had good representation in football and improvement in the school's academic ranking. It was not viewed that way in all quarters.

The records for Terry's teams were 7-3-0 in 1957, and 6-4-0 in 1958. That's all it took to arouse the alumni and to tighten the hold on their wallets. By the next year, Terry was on his way out. It became obvious that the program of this young coach did not fulfill the expectations of the Notre Dame alumni. Father Hesburgh initially resisted their demands but eventually he and Father Joyce and the Board of Athletics gave way. The alumni worked to rout Terry with their financial and other pressures when his teams failed to live up to the legendary standards of the "Domers" who saw only the won-lost records of those years. They wanted action immediately. Ignoring the effects of the limitations placed on the program, they would not give Terry any further time to become the mature coach of whom so much was demanded.

Terry's finish at ND was a long, painful, lingering episode in the minds of many. To be informed just before the Christmas holiday, as Terry was, that he had the opportunity to either resign or be released from his cherished position rankled him and many of us, but the die was cast. Terry had too much Irish pride to resign. If Notre Dame no longer wanted him, let them be the ones to bear the responsibility for his departure. And so it was.

That was his fate, despite the records he had established during his years at Notre Dame. His release created a foul taste in the mouths of many of those shouting the praises of Our Lady's University. Terry had brought fame to the school with his play throughout his athletic career at Notre Dame, and most specifically, against the powerful Army team in 1947. As a coach, he had also won fame and recognition for Notre Dame in the victory over the powerful, long-unbeaten Oklahoma team, breaking the "Sooners" string of 47 consecutive winning games on November 16, 1957 by a score of 7-0.

These successes were soon forgotten, and even today, there are

Notre Dame breaks Oklahoma's winning streak of 47 consecutive games under Coach Terry Brennan.

those who minimize Terry's achievements. His coaching record cannot be evaluated by comparison with the records of others. Terry learned of an article evaluating his years at Notre Dame which appeared in a Notre Dame publication a few years ago.

He wrote a letter to the Notre Dame Magazine in February of 2010 in response to certain statements that had been made in the magazine viewing his coaching record unfavorably and with degrading insinuations on comparison with others at Notre Dame.

Terry pointed out in his letter that football was played under different NCAA rules in the 1950s such as the "one platoon" system, in which the same group of men played on defense as well as offense. In earlier years, as well as in later years, "free substitution" was allowed, whereby men could be removed from the game and later returned to the game. There were advantages with this "free substitution" system, as it permitted more specialists in the game. Players were on the field for shorter periods, keeping players fresher. This system also allowed the substitution of entire platoons drilled in offense or defense.

The University had different policies regarding football in the 1950s. Academic standards at Notre Dame were dramatically increased, and compliance had become mandatory. Notre Dame required the College Board Entrance Exam (now the SAT) used only by Ivy League Schools at that time. This limited recruiting to the student capable of these higher standards. The NCAA had no uniform minimum academic standards for eligibility.

Terry wrote, "At the start of my coaching years at Notre Dame, the school unilaterally cut our scholarships in half. Freshmen were not allowed to play at any school during my coaching years. The other national football programs did allow redshirting and transfers. Notre Dame did not."

"Now, all Division I programs require SAT exams, minimum

TERENCE P. BRENNAN
1731D WILDBERRY
GLENVIEW, IL 60025

Mr. Lou Somogyi
Senior Editor
Blue and Gold Illustrated
P.O. Box 1007
Notre Dame, Indiana 46556

February 20, 201(

Dear Mr. Somogyi:

Someone recently sent me the article "Haven't We Been Here Already?" you wrote from the November 30 issue of the Blue and Gold magazine comparing my coaching career at Notre Dame with that of Charlie Weis. The answer to your question is a resounding "no." You are trying to compare two different eras 50 years apart. The two eras played under different NCAA rules such as the "one platoon" system in the 1950s vs. free substitution now. The university also had different policies regarding football under Fr. Hesburgh the university president in the 1950s than it does under the current administration. I have nothing against Charlie, but I don't want to be compared with him.

Let me offer a more complete accounting of the facts.

Because of decisions made by the administration in the 1950s and my predecessor, Frank Leahy, I was never on an even playing field with my opponents academically or with scholarships. As you point out, academic standards at Notre Dame were increased—dramatically. Beginning with my tenure as head coach, Notre Dame required the college entrance board exam (now called the SAT) out of Princeton for entrance to Notre Dame. The only schools that used that exam at the time were Notre Dame and the Ivy League. There were no uniform minimum academic standards for eligibility at the national level.

Also, at the start of my coaching years at ND, the school unilaterally cut our scholarships in half. In Frank Leahy's last year, the administration put forth a policy where scholarships would be 80 over a 4 year period. At the time, every other football program in the country was bringing in well in excess of that number. As usual, Leahy ignored the rules and brought in over 30 players which didn't leave much for the next 3 years. Also the group he brought in were seniors in 1956. It wasn't the strongest recruiting class.

While freshman were not allowed to play at any school during my coaching years, the other national football programs did allow redshirting and transfers. Notre Dame did not. Also Leahy, who was angry with Notre Dame, took his wrath out on me through the press. As I said before, we were not on a level playing field with our opponents.

like my situation, for the last five years Charlie and Notre Dame have enjoyed an even playing field with their opponents. Now all of the Division 1 programs require the SAT exam or its equivalent for entrance to their schools, and the NCAA Clearinghouse assures at least a minimum standard of academic eligibility. The number of scholarships is now set by the NCAA, not by individual schools, at 85 over 4

Terry Brennan's letter responds to the criticism of his period as Head Coach of Notre Dame football.

academic standards are set, the number of scholarships is set at 85 over 4 years by the NCAA, and redshirting and transfers are allowed. The one platoon system has been eliminated. We were at a disadvantage compared to other schools," wrote Terry.

"We prided ourselves on playing the toughest programs in the country. In 1958, my final year as coach, we played five teams in the top 20, including the 2nd, 3rd, and 11th ranked teams in the final AP poll for that year. We finished the year 6-4 and were ranked 17th in the country."

During Terry's tenure, Notre Dame finished in the top ten in the AP poll in 1954, 1955, and 1957, and ranked 10th in 1958 and 17th in 1959.

When one sees these figures in broad daylight, most of us agree that it should have been acceptable, especially when one considers the limitations placed on the football program and the priorities given to academics at the time. Further, the University had chosen a coach competent at his level of experience and maturity to meet the limited expectations of the school. But remember the alumni, and this is Notre Dame.

By 1959, Terry's support by the Board of Athletics and members of the Congregation of Holy Cross had weakened. Terry was released from his position as head football coach.

A new coach was to be found. The powers who had prevailed were now seeking a coach who was more seasoned, experienced, and proven. Why not go all the way? Don't stop at the college ranks. Get a man from the pros. He would have all the answers to major league football. That's what Notre Dame decided.

Their search found him: a pro coach, a native of South Bend, successful in the pro ranks, one who had served as head coach with the old Chicago Cardinals in 1953 and with the Washington

Redskins in 1954-58. Here was a man who was all business, no foolishness, all work and, hopefully, capable of success at the college level. Notre Dame would present a football team to the world representing Notre Dame well, a team of which the University could be proud, and one that would bring honor to the school. The University's goal of a higher education would be most visible, and sportsmanship and sports would be recognized for their real values in the development of strong and worthy men.

Coach Joseph Kuharich
1959-1962

JOE KUHARICH was their man. With his background and with the number of scholarships offered having been restored to normal, the body Notre Dame welcomed him, with anticipation of the huge success that should now surely come. Instead, they found themselves with a man who did not relate to the youths he was to coach, nor they to him.

The coach himself was a stoic, self-sufficient man, who was not troubled with his inability to communicate with his players. He had good assistant coaches who could do their job and communicate as well. Neither did he establish good rapport with the physicians attending the team. He made it their primary goal to return the injured player to the field as soon as possible. Our personal goal was to see that the players received the best of care and rehabilitation to enable them to do their best for the team.

His reluctant cooperation in medical decisions was probably best illustrated in the case of Myron Pottios, one of the fine players recruited by Terry Brennan and who was a stalwart of Kuharich's

Coach Joseph Kuharich is recruited from the ranks of professional football to become the Head Football Coach at Notre Dame.

team. "Mo" played the position of guard on the 1960 team until he suffered a severe injury to his knee. An X-ray showed the bony structures of the knee to be normal. I examined the man and found that Mo had suffered injuries to the anterior cruciate ligament, the medial structures, and the posterior cruciate ligament of the knee. Surgical repair was indicated. I had to go to the coach and explain what had happened to Mo and what was to be done.

I finished my day's work and went out to practice, which was being conducted in the stadium that day. The coach was sitting in the stands, about thirty rows up, on about the forty-yard line, observing the workouts. After a brief greeting and discussion, he asked why surgery was necessary on the player who had been injured only yesterday. He had been informed that the X-ray was negative. This player had been able to limp off the field. The coach was of the opinion that the player could not have been injured so badly if he was able to walk off the field. He had seen many knees injured but "they didn't need surgery so soon. Surgery was not usually successful anyway in returning a player to the lineup," he said. He felt that the player might get better in a week or two without surgery. He did not want to give up a player who would not return soon if surgery were done. "Why don't we wait and see if the knee really needed surgery? Couldn't surgery wait until after the season was over?"

In discussing this with Coach Kuharich, I realized that the coach did not understand the problem. In his mind, he was lumping all knee injuries together, not separating "apples from oranges." Here again was the old problem of convincing the coach that you were doing a proper job and that the knee would do best if surgery were done early. I mentioned that if he saw the knee as I would find it in surgery, he would understand why surgery was indicated at this time. The coach said he would like to see that. I suggested that he witness the surgery so he could better understand the situation. He accepted the invitation and the following day, we met in surgery at St. Joseph Hospital.

He was given scrub clothes, mask, gown, and booties, our usual O.R. outfits, and was warned to avoid touching our gowns or any operating equipment while in the operating room. I had received permission from Myron and the Operating Room Supervisor, Miss Mann, to go as planned.

The coach entered the room with me. I spoke a few words of assurance to Mo and directed the anesthesiologist to proceed. The patient was anesthetized. A tourniquet was applied, and a sterile scrub and "prep" was done on the leg, from ankle to groin. The leg was then draped outside of the sheets with sterile wrapping, and the operative field was covered with sterile drapes. The tourniquet was now inflated. My assistant was Dr. George Colip, the University physician at that time. The scrub nurse was at her table, prepared to do her work with us.

As I prepared to make the incision, the circulating nurse spoke to the coach who was standing in a corner of the room. She advised him that he could come closer to the operating table to view the operation, but she also warned him not to touch anyone or anything. She placed him about a foot behind my right shoulder. I too was conscious of the need to avoid sudden movements, which might cause contact and contamination of our sterile area.

As I made the incision, there was a sudden gush of blood that had collected in the joint—nothing unusual about that in an injury like this. As I dissected further, I came down on the medial side of the joint, where the capsule had been avulsed from the tibia. The medial collateral ligament was torn near its distal attachments, and its deeper layer was avulsed from the tibia. The meniscus was torn from the posterior capsule at its margin for a short distance. The anterior cruciate ligament was avulsed from its femoral attachment. The posterior cruciate ligament was torn in a long oblique manner leaving the more posterior segment attached to the tibia and the proximal segment attached to the femur. This latter tear made this a more severe injury than the usual one. These tears had occurred in a somewhat irregular manner, leaving frayed tissues dangling in the joint.

As I was pointing out this pathology to the coach, the nurse

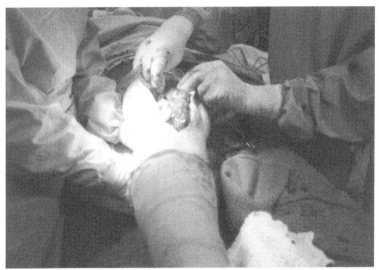

A view of a knee in surgery, much like that of Myron Pottios, after cleansing and debridement.

noticed the coach's manner to be disinterested. He appeared somewhat grey and shaky. She quickly had a chair for him and, as she suggested, he sat with his head down for a short time. After a brief interval, he suddenly recalled that he had an appointment waiting at his office. We understood. The nurse helped him back to the dressing room. He was okay. Our credibility was established. We continued the surgery.

The joint was irrigated, cleansing it of blood. Frayed tissues were trimmed. The meniscus was sutured to its normal location at the posterior capsule. The posterior cruciate ligament was repaired, suturing it front to back with mattress sutures. The anterior cruciate ligament was repaired with sutures, but the reattachment would be questionable, and so it was reinforced with a structure to replace the ligament with tissue from the patellar tendon and tissue from the front of the patella and with adjacent fibers of the quadriceps tendon. This was completed, leaving it attached distally, and fashioning and sewing it into a tube-like structure. It was left attached to the tibia and was now displaced into a groove chiseled into the front of the joint to enable its positioning in the area close to the base of the still-attached normal anterior cruciate ligament (Lam's modification of the Jones operation). Sutures were then passed through the tube's proximal end. Through a small incision, a hole was drilled through the lateral condyle of the femur to exit in the inter-condylar area at the area of the normal attachment of the anterior cruciate ligament. The leading sutures were then passed through the drill hole from inside to the outside of the lateral condyle. The sutures were drawn tight to put the new ligament under tension. They were then sutured into the condyle through another smaller drill hole, and were tied under tension. The joint capsule was sutured and the layers of the medial collateral ligament were re-attached at their near-normal anatomic sites. The joint was again irrigated. The tourniquet was deflated. Bleeding was controlled with cautery, and the wound was closed in layers. A plaster splint was applied. The patient's condition was good on leaving the operating room.

The cast was changed when the sutures were removed ten days postoperatively. All casting was removed at six weeks and physical therapy was started, followed a few weeks later by other rehabilitation efforts.

Myron, like many other players who underwent knee ligament repairs, underwent extensive post-op rehabilitation. Even so, many were likely to have some slight degree of instability of that knee, mainly from loss of the full stability of the anterior cruciate ligament. Medial-lateral instability of a few millimeters on stressing the knee could be overcome with strong thigh muscles—if the instability did not exceed a few millimeters. However, the loss of antero-posterior stability could be overcome to a lesser degree. This was especially likely to manifest itself when combined with rotary stresses on the knee. The results of surgery for anterior cruciate injuries are much superior with today's techniques than were those of this earlier era. Nevertheless, some of these men did return to their sport, as did Myron Pottios, Ray Lemek, and others. That was dependent on their intense rehabilitation of the muscles controlling the knee joint, as well as the individual's fortitude and determination.

Myron did well post-operatively and did return to play at Notre Dame his senior year. He was then selected by the pros and played with Pittsburgh in 1961, and from 1963-65; with the Rams from 1966-70; and with Washington from 1971-74.

When Terry Brennan came out to visit me in Palm Desert on several occasions during the winter months in the last few years, we would look up "Mo," who now had his residence there. He indicated that the knee was fine, never gave him a bit of trouble. That was either "macho" or just a means to feed my ego because, in 2010, he informed us that his knee had been replaced—not an unusual story with these athletes' joints after the beating they take. Yet almost every one of them says they would do it all over again.

They understood that they were taking these risks when they decided to play football, but of course, like most of us, it is seen to be one of those things that happen to the other fellow. The athletes were willing to take those chances; and, if misfortune did occur, they worked hard if there was any possibility of returning to the game.

Coach Kuharich had a modicum of success, but not that degree of success expected of a coach at Notre Dame. He did have his trials and setbacks, including the loss of Pottios for that year.

Another came with the loss of Les Traver, a gifted athlete who was cut down by a block that tore his knee joint severely.

Traver was a senior, so his college career ended at that time. He did not enter the ranks of the pros. Recent communication from him indicated that he has successfully participated in many other sports, including tennis, basketball, and others since then. Although he is now experiencing symptoms that are probably those of early arthritis, he has not required any further surgery.

A negative in Kuharich's personality was the inability to communicate with the alumni, with his team, and with others.

Les Traver is blocked below the knee. This was legal at the time.

This left much to be desired. His inability at enhancing public relations was a negative. As a coach, he was at a loss on how to work with these young college players. These elements, which were lacking in his makeup, were important elements of the head-coaching job.

When it was found that the coach chosen by the school did not have the charisma to inspire players, and whose coaching was suited better for the mature and developed player rather than the developing young player, and when his recruiting results, which mirrored the success of the program, all became negative factors at ND, there was trouble afoot again.

A closer view of the injury to Les Traver's knee

Such was the short-lived tenure of Coach Kuharich, whose record of 17 wins to 23 losses over a four-year period doomed him. The alumni were still demanding a better showing of their beloved football team—and they would get it. The coach made a quick decision. He would leave.

Many factors combined to influence Coach Kuharich to make the sudden, untimely decision to "abandon ship," which he did. He probably saw the handwriting on the wall, which spoke of terminating his reign. He had found other opportunities open to him at the time, in the ranks of the officials in pro football. He no doubt evaluated the situation perfectly and took off.

Now, with his abrupt exit, and with the new season close at hand, ND had no time or opportunity to make a thorough search for a new head coach.

Coach Hugh Devore
1945 and 1963

HUGH DEVORE was an old standby at Notre Dame. Hugh had an extensive array of credentials, having coached at several colleges and several of the "pro" teams.

He had been head coach at Notre Dame in 1945 while Coach Leahy was in the Navy. Hughie had a 7-2-1 record that year. With the sudden departure of Coach Kuharich, Hugh Devore was appointed head football coach.

Everyone, including Hughie, knew that this appointment was a temporary assignment. The appointment took him by surprise, just as it did everyone else. Hughie was not prepared for the position of head coach with this team. It was still in the process of

Coach Hugh Devore

developing as a team. He was in over his head, and he knew it. He did the best he could, but it was a dismal season—only two wins. The players and other coaches were soon aware of his frailties. They did not demonstrate the respect usually given to a man in his position. ND football again suffered until they found the right coach for the job.

I had almost no contact with Coach Devore. He followed his agenda and left the medical program alone. He had his share of misfortune too. He lost an excellent running back to the auto accident, which was mentioned earlier. Don Hogan suffered severe injuries to his hip and pelvis earlier that year when his car was involved in a collision with another vehicle. Don had a good year at halfback the prior season and could have been a great help to the 1963 team. He was ruled out of participation after a brief trial of function.

Outside of this circle of events and persons, it was obvious to the football world that ND was in trouble. Rumors had quickly developed suggesting that Hughie would not be there for long. This would be followed by good news.

During this interval, there was an ambitious, brilliant, still-young coach, who was moving up the line with a successful career coaching football. He was now coaching at one of the elite schools, so he already knew what might lay ahead at Notre Dame in terms of recruiting, demanding academics, work ethics, moral codes, and discipline. Above all, he knew football and men. He demanded the best of himself and of those around him—coaches, trainers, medical staff, and others associated with his program. He had the ability to get the best out of them; and the same was true with his players.

Coach Ara Parseghian
1964-1974

Coach Ara Parseghian

THE MAN, ARA PARSEGHIAN, was aware of the rumors that ND could be seeking a new coach in the near future. His teams at Northwestern University had played at Notre Dame every other year, and, whereas Northwestern had lost regularly under other coaches, Ara's teams had beaten Notre Dame on the four successive occasions that they competed in South Bend. He took it upon himself to make cautious inquiry and in doing so, he demonstrated interest in the job at ND, should it materialize. This led to clandestine meetings between Ara and the few at Notre Dame who were involved in these machinations, namely Father Joyce, and finally, Father Hesburgh. They were successful at keeping the meetings silent until everyone was ready for the welcomed announcement that Ara was to be the new head coach of football at Notre Dame.

The appointment of Ara Parseghian was a surprise to most of us. He was having success at Northwestern. He was a Protestant, and one would have thought this would be a deterrent to hiring him. There was little to suggest that he was a candidate for the position. The appointment at ND was considered a most prestigious one with the history of ND over the years as a gridiron great. It was a plum in that way, if not financially. Ultimately, Ara was drawn from the shadows and identified as the new head coach.

Ara's coming was a boon to Notre Dame. The days of triumph were to be restored. It was the "second coming" as far as the student body was concerned. They not only warmed to him immediately, but they endowed him with metaphysical powers, as witnessed by the entire student body in the stands chanting, "Ara, stop the rain! Ara, stop the rain!" at one point during the season.

The team also responded positively, as did the recruiting of new talent. Changes were made in the assignment of existing players.

In his first season on the job, Ara demonstrated his perceptive abilities when he elevated John Huarte to first-string quarterback, whereas John had been rated as the third-string quarterback the previous year. This assignment led to Huarte's selection as the Heisman Trophy winner in 1964. Ara was given credit for not only seeing and developing the hidden talent on the team, but he proved early his ability to evaluate his players' potential abilities. He transferred numerous players from one position to another where they proved themselves even better suited than they had been theretofore. The Townsend boys were an example. Willie was shifted from halfback to end, and Mike from cornerback to safety. They showcased their talents well in their new positions.

There is one other point that seemed obvious to me from my position. It was that Ara, like Leahy, had the good fortune and judgment to avail himself of experienced and good coaches who were available at that time. He gathered a group of assistant coaches who knew football and knew how to instill into the players the right way to play their part of the game. All this, in turn, reflected on the head coach who reigned over all in this effort. Here, then, was a highly competent group of coaches working together to restore the glory that had been Notre Dame's.

The entire program seemed to change under Ara. It was better structured and organized. Practice sessions were run by the clock. Coaches and physicians were all accountable to Ara. He had his finger on every detail. He ran the program efficiently. As a result, everyone knew just where he stood, and everyone then recognized his accountability for his assignment, how it was to be done, and when. Hope was in the air.

My work under Ara was initially a challenge. He had to know exactly what was going on. He was inquisitive, deeply questioning. With his direct approach and beetle-browed, dark-eyed appearance in face-to-face meetings, you knew you had better

Head Football Coach Ara Parseghian with fellow coaches, Joe Yonto on the left, and George Kelly on the right

get to the point quickly and succinctly. He was smart. He was not only intelligent, but he had the street smarts too for working with the bunch of young guys he inherited. He saw through the problems and guises that presented themselves. And, in time, you learned that he was fair. That was demonstrated well in the case of several of his players who found themselves in trouble. They were accused of rape—wrongfully, they said. Nevertheless, they were dismissed from school and the football program. He agreed with the administration that it was a proper disciplinary move. At the end of that year of penance, four of the six young men, having paid the penalty, were permitted to return to school and their scholarships. They were reinstated into the football program. He gave them another chance.

His inquisitive nature created an interesting situation for us. He was smart enough to understand the changes that were developing in the management of knee injuries. He wanted to know more.

Harry Long suffered severe injuries to the ligaments of his knee in Ara's first game as head coach at Notre Dame. Harry played the position of right end and was injured in a play that led to a touchdown. Despite that severe injury, Harry lined up for the point after touchdown play. After that, he hobbled off that end of the field and back to the Notre Dame sideline, before giving in to the pain. I was not at that game, but I examined him when he was brought back to school. The ACL and medial ligaments were torn. I did surgery on him the next day. The eventual result was good. Harry regained his position as end for the next two years.

I have had other players who also played one or more plays after such an injury, so the ability to walk off the field does not indicate the degree of injury.

The day came when I had to inform Ara of the need for surgery for ligament injuries to the knee of another one of his players. The man had undergone X-ray studies with normal findings. Ara wanted to know how, then, did I determine the need for surgery. I explained that I did it by stressing the ligaments to determine if the structure was or was not intact.

"How do you do that?" he asked. I took his knee and showed him a few of the maneuvers that were done to decide this. He thought he understood but asked if I could show him on that patient in question, so we arranged that for the next day.

He came down to the trainer's room. I had the patient on the examining table and showed Ara the slightly angled position of the knee for the Lachman test, the right-angle position for the anterior and posterior draw signs, and the position of the leg for varus and valgus thrusts on the knee to show the stability of these ligaments. I also explained the need to compare the normal knee with the affected knee. He was attentive and immediately asked, "Can I do that? Let me try it."

"Certainly." I let him do it, and with a little coaching, he experienced the laxity of the anterior cruciate and the medial collateral ligaments of the knee in this case.

This convinced him, and I think he was also a little proud of himself for doing the exam to our mutual satisfaction. I believe it also better satisfied him that this was indeed an unstable knee. He understood the need for surgery. Again, I had established my credibility, passed the test, the need to prove myself. We did this on a number of other occasions. He seemed to like the idea of being able to diagnose and experience the laxity of the knees so injured.

There was one other aspect to this. In my opinion, there was some kind of a wall broken down between the coaching and the medical teams by this open and frank communication with Ara. It registered well enough with him that he requested that I take care of the team's orthopaedic problems both spring and fall. He did not like the idea of having different physicians seeing the players from one season to the next. Until then, the program had been shared with Dr. Denham's associates. Now that changed.

I felt that I had his confidence when his son Michael developed back pain. Michael had been an outstanding high school player— a halfback who carried and ran the ball with the best of them. He had also made the team at Notre Dame, not on the family name, but on his performance. He saw considerable action at his position with the team, but in time, he owned up to back pain that had been nagging him for some time and was getting worse. X-rays were normal; however, there had been reports over the last few years of "stress" fractures in the low back area, just as they also occurred in other areas of the body—feet, ankles, legs, and elsewhere. But the X-rays of Michael's back did not reveal stress fractures.

More recent literature reported that the actual fracture would be preceded by a "stress reaction" on bone scans. This is a

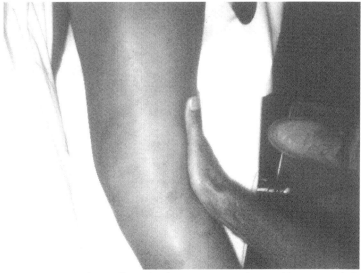

Demonstration of the effect of valgus stress on a knee with torn medial collateral ligament and capsular structures, and torn anterior cruciate ligament

pathologic state in which the early and developing stress fracture is preceded by changes in the internal structure of bone at the area of abnormal stress, where changes in bone metabolism take place. This could be identified by radioactive studies, during which a small dose of radioactive material is injected into the body. The material concentrates in the area of heightened bone metabolism, creating changes in the bone that are then visible to X-ray. The test on Michael was positive.

Such stress reactions and fractures could heal with rest when diagnosed early. Otherwise, they would progress to fractures; and in this area of the lower back, it was found to be the cause of a condition known as spondylolysis. This could then proceed to a more advanced condition in which there is actual displacement of one vertebra in relation to the adjoining vertebra, spondylolisthesis.

Back pain was usually the presenting symptom and was often disabling. Michael's stress reaction was diagnosed early enough that we could hope for healing, but rest meant no physical exertion, no strain on the low back area. Translation: rest, and no football. Michael was as smart as his dad was, and both agreed that Michael should stop playing. He did, and the stress reaction eventually subsided over a period of months. It healed and the pain was gone. I don't know how much this had to do with his subsequent interests and decisions, but Michael went on to finish his education and entered medical school. He is now a well-respected orthopaedic surgeon himself, in Tucson, Arizona.

These experiences brought Coach Parseghian and me to a better understanding of each other's position. We developed a lasting friendship. Ara had, and still has, a good sense of humor behind that foreboding and demanding heavily browed mask. Today we laugh, talking of the days when he was examining knees with me.

Many of us are well aware of the fact that there have been several times in Ara's life when there was no laughter. Michael and his wife Cindy had the misfortune of losing three children to Niemann-Pick Disease—a rare, genetic abnormality in the storage of fat cells in various tissues of the body, leading to certain death. Ara and his wife, Katie, endured this with son Michael and his wife, watching these children die of this untreatable condition as they approached adolescence—a condition about which so little is known and for which there is no known treatment of value. Meanwhile, Ara and Katie continued to wage a battle in support of their daughter Karen who ultimately died of her disease, Multiple Sclerosis.

One would think that a man who has achieved such success in

life, as Ara has, would be entitled to his full measure of happiness and the good life, but that doesn't necessarily follow. They pay their dues like anyone else. Of course, Ara doesn't take things lying down. He has been active on the National Board of the Multiple Sclerosis Society, and he has founded a research program, hoping to find a cure for Niemann-Pick Disease—research that likely will also benefit a number of other closely related disorders.

There was an interesting episode in our history with Ara. It was in the course of the 1966 season. ND quarterback Terry Hanratty had been having a great year, about to set new records at Notre Dame, when he injured his knee in the classic 10-10 battle at Michigan State. Sure enough, it was unstable. With Southern Cal still on the schedule, Ara was eager to keep Hanratty going. Somewhere along the way, he broke ranks and suggested that we get another opinion. I agreed and mentioned that I could probably get Dr. Joe Godfrey, orthopaedic surgeon to the Buffalo Bills, to give us a second opinion. Dr. Godfrey had been to the game that week and had stayed over to visit his son, Bill, a Notre Dame student at the time. Ara agreed.

I located Dr. Godfrey and he consented to see Hanratty. On examining Terry, he agreed that surgery was indicated and he had me take X-rays comparing the two knees with a technique placing stress on the injured ligaments, which revealed the widening of the affected joint on the injured side. Here was visible proof that Ara accepted, and Terry was added to the list of men injured and coming to surgery after that "shoot-out" at Michigan State.

There were others injured in that game as well. "Rocky" Bleier and George Goeddeke, both had torn knee ligaments requiring surgery. They too were "paying their dues," part of the cost of that great game which made us National Champions for 1966 with a record of nine wins and one tie, no losses.

Another of Ara's players who incurred serious injury was George Kunz. It was in a game at Northwestern University that Kunz suffered a serious injury to his left knee when he was "clipped" while pursuing the runner on a punt return. This required surgery for the "terrible triad": torn ACL, medial meniscus, and medial

Terry Hanratty, our quarterback in 1966 until he was injured in the Michigan State Game

capsule and collateral ligaments. The result was good enough that he was a unanimous choice for All-American honors. He not only played two more years at ND after that, but he then went on to play eight years of professional football. A recent conversation

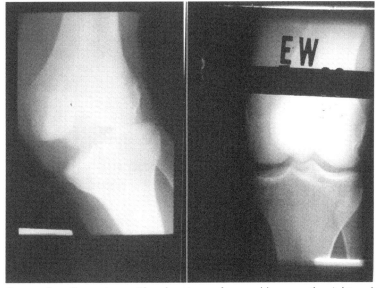

Comparison X-ray views with valus stress of normal knee on the right and severely injured knee on the left

with him revealed that he did undergo removal of a torn lateral meniscus in that knee during his post-graduate career. Otherwise, the knee was holding up well. No replacement, such as is often the final story with these knees. The results of surgery on these knees that made them good enough to return them to a career in athletics is very satisfying to a surgeon and his rehabilitation team. No small credit is also due the athlete whose determination and endurance are the final and most important factors in such recovery and achievement. I believe Himself has a hand in it too. George Kunz was the second man chosen in the NFL Draft his senior year.

He played with Atlanta from 1969-74, and with Baltimore 1975-77 and 1980. (See supplement number one re other Notre Dame players in the ranks of the professionals following surgery.)

Coaches do not like to hear that surgery is necessary on their players. It is not empathy alone for the players, but the coaches are also aware that the player will be lost from the lineup for varying periods of time after surgery. Coaches also recall those knee operations of the past when it seemed that little good resulted from such surgery. The more exact diagnosis and surgical methods of today ensure that the surgery will be appropriate for that condition.

George Kunz

In recent times, coaches are aware that through surgery they may regain a functional athlete who otherwise would have been lost. This is true not only with knees but with many other conditions about the shoulders, elbows, back, etc.

However, even successful surgery does not guarantee the return of that player to competition. Tony Capers, an offensive lineman in 1968, was an example. He was a big man—well built, strong, fast, smart, and a versatile football player. Among his talents was his ability to kick the ball. As a freshman, he was destined to be our kickoff man.

In the opening game of that year, the teams lined up for the kick. The referee and Tony exchanged signals. Tony signaled the team, and he ran forward to kick the ball, and kick it he did! It sailed to the end zone. Unfortunately, as Tony came down on his foot in the process of the kickoff, he felt a snap at the lower end of his calf, and the leg collapsed beneath him. He had very little pain, but there was marked weakness of the foot and ankle. The diagnosis was evident immediately. He had completely torn the Achilles tendon—the stout cord just beneath the skin behind the ankle. This was enough to finish him for the season. Surgery was necessary. The tendon was successfully repaired.

Tony cooperated well. He wore the cast for twelve weeks. The first cast extended above the knee. This was removed after the first six weeks, and a short leg cast was applied. The foot, in both instances, was pointed downward to relieve tension on the repair. Thereafter, light touch weight bearing was allowed for two weeks with an elevated heel, which again placed the foot pointed downward. Later, light weight bearing and then full weight bearing was allowed on the foot, using a shoe with an elevated heel. This heel acted to diminish the tension on the strengthening Achilles. Such a tendon repair requires time for the fibers of the tendon to

Tony Capers

bridge the gap and become the strong, mature tendon necessary for its functions. Tony was at this early stage of full weight bearing and doing well when fate intervened.

Tony had found some activity as a disc jockey at the University's radio station during his period of healing and was developing a fan following of his own. He was a popular guy. He was also working at his studies, trying to keep up his grades.

He was surprised one day as he sat in the station looking over the next disc he would put on the air, sitting astride the tall stool that disc jockeys seem to prefer. There was a commotion outside his studio. Suddenly the door flew open, and in stormed his lady friend, screaming and shouting, calling him names he hadn't heard before, giving it to him straight about what a double-crossing bum he was after all she had done for him—a two-timer, a good for nothing piece of tripe who wasn't worth a penny, you #&^?*&#!! Then she suddenly went for Tony. He jumped off his stool and came down on his foot only to experience again that ominous SNAP! behind his ankle. He managed to get out of harm's way and she was calmed after a while. But Tony's tendon was torn again!

We were back in surgery a few days later. The procedure now was technically more involved, requiring a flap of tissue to be reflected from the back of his calf muscle. This was imbricated with the freshened torn ends of the Achilles tendon, reinforcing it with this fresh and strong tissue.

The repair of such a scarred tendon would take an even longer period of time than before. Tony had already lost a lot of time in school during these surgical and recovery sessions. This did interfere with his studies. Tony did not make it back to school the next year. He had the potential to make it in the NFL from all I had heard about him. Tony left school and transferred his further care to his local orthopod. Unfortunately, I lost track of him, but I understand he went on to a career in the pros and radio.

Ara's career at Notre Dame had placed him in the top tier of the school's legendary coaches. His team went on again in 1973 to become National Champions: eleven wins, no losses or ties. His teams accomplished this through painstaking work and his coaching. Throughout all this time, he demonstrated the character, intelligence, ethics, and morality of a winner. I don't know of any fault we could find with him. Reminds you of that old Irish ballad whose words are: "It's a name that a shame never has been connected with..." He is a man worthy of the admiration he has gained from those who know him, as well as those who do not. He had earned a rightful place in their estimations, putting him above many others, who have yet to travel that road—fame—which betrays so many on their spasmodic journey through life. He was a role model for many of us—an icon and a leader.

But it can get pretty hot in the kitchen, and Ara was starting to feel it. He was conscientious about being well prepared for games, and he blamed himself when the team failed.

I recall the game with Southern Cal in 1974. The score was 24-0 in favor of Notre Dame, until just before the first half ended when USC scored. Then USC scored again at the beginning of the second half of the game. Our margin was disappearing—and it did. The game ended 24-55 in favor of Southern Cal.

There were rumors, unfounded, that something serious had happened in the locker room at halftime, affecting the game. Not so, although one of our "bad-boy" halfbacks was found to be phoning his girlfriend out in the hallway during halftime. This did not fit Area's concept of maintaining focus on the game. Word was passed down to the young man and the matter was closed.

Ara was still brooding over the loss as we boarded the plane to return to South Bend. I allowed the players, coaches and others to get on the plane before I boarded. There was one seat left—next to Ara. Apparently, the others knew that this was not the time to be sitting with him. We took off, Ara still brooding. I tried to make some light conversation, only to hear him say to himself, "What did I miss? What more should I have prepared for? How could I have foreseen that?" He glummed up. Another attempt by me elicited the same self-deprecatory response from him. We spent the rest of the trip in silence. "Heavy lies the head that wears the crown."

NATIONAL CHAMPIONS
1966, 1973

Ara's record set a benchmark for the coaches who would follow him at Notre Dame. Success would be based on a winning record and other factors meeting Notre Dame's standards, such as those involved in recruiting, academics, and high moral and ethical behavior. These standards are not easy to keep but are demanded by those, especially at ND, who place a high value on the integrity and spirit of college athletics. There are many programs that fail this test.

Coach Parseghian's record at Notre Dame stood up well against that of Coach Frank Leahy. However, comparing Leahy's record of four National Championships in eleven years with Ara's record of

Coach Parseghian receives national recognition.

two championships (1966, 1973) in eleven years is as impossible as comparing apples and oranges. The times were different in many ways, especially in numbers of players and scholarships, academic requirements, and rules of the game.

RETIREMENT

Ara felt the stress as his career had become more and more demanding. Some of the problems were no doubt related to the pressures of the position he had attained with hard work, long hours, and his dedication to the job and to the team. As blood pressure and cardiac symptoms arose, he gave serious consideration to the importance of his life's goals and satisfaction. When things became bad enough, he carefully weighed the advice given him by various specialists and friends, and he wisely decided that there was more to life than football. The severe involvement of his daughter with Multiple Sclerosis, leading ultimately to her death, and the knowledge that three of his grandchildren were destined to die of Niemann-Pick Disease entered into his decision. They needed him too; and he couldn't let them down by continuing his high-pressure lifestyle as a coach, which could well lead to a suddenly disabling or even fatal condition if he continued coaching. Ara was a very smart man in so many ways. He had proven it in sports

National Champions, 1973

and in business. He showed it again by making the right decision. Quit while you're ahead, and take time for a life of your own with your wife and family. He did.

Ara and his wife, Katie, enter retirement to enjoy the peace and quiet of a more normal life.

Ara had advised the University of his decision in ample time for them to make a search for his replacement. With the retirement of Coach Parseghian, the search for a new coach turned again to the pro ranks, to a man who was not much appreciated as coach of the Green Bay Packers. Dan Devine, a coach with an oft-proven record of success at the college game, was to be the new coach of the Fighting Irish.

Coach Dan Devine
1975-1980

DAN DEVINE was well respected in his profession, but he had not been happy at Green Bay, or possibly, it was the other way around. His record there was 25 wins, 27 losses, and 4 ties.

Dan Devine's records as a college coach at Arizona State (27-3-1) and Missouri (93-37-7) were outstanding. He obviously knew how to work with the younger athletes, and he knew what it took to achieve success in that company.

The new coach had a temperament that differed from that of Ara's. He was much more reserved—not an enthusiastic, outgoing personality. However, he was serious about his football and very knowledgeable. He adapted readily to his new environment, and we, the medical staff, had less difficulty adapting to him than we had experienced with some of the other coaches. His quiet manner encouraged easy discussion of problem situations. Rarely was there disagreement with my actions. On only one occasion did this become an issue between us. I learned at that time that he was not without his wiles.

One of our athletes had suffered a neck injury in pre-season practice and X-rays revealed a slight compression of the upper plate of the sixth cervical vertebral body. There was no mention of fracture. However, my review of the X-rays revealed that they also showed a slight anterior displacement of the fifth vertebra on the sixth, associated with an increase in the spacing between the spinous processes of these two vertebrae. Examination of the man revealed pain and tenderness at this level of the spine, and pain localized at this area. To me this meant that the upper vertebra had started to dislocate anteriorly, tearing the posterior spinal ligaments, thereby weakening this area of the cervical spine. This slight depression of the upper vertebral plate is seen frequently in older individuals (the result of normal changes), but not at this football player's age. These were not remarkable changes—not like a clean-cut fracture or dislocation of the spine—but with definite evidence of weakening of the structures at that level. This would heal safely with six to eight weeks of bracing but, until then, a second injury from a particular angle could result in further displacement of the vertebra, and there was even the possibility that such additional injury could lead to serious neurological consequences.

I disqualified the man for contact workouts and arranged to brace his neck, but I also encouraged him to maintain his conditioning while his neck healed and stabilized. On discussing the injury with

Coach Dan Devine and the captains of his first Notre Dame Team, 1975, Jim Stock (on left) and Ed Bauer (on right).

Coach Devine, I mentioned that the routine X-ray report had not indicated this as a serious injury. We did not yet have bone scans, which could have told us more. My interpretation of the X-rays suggested a more serious injury than reported by the radiologist. The coach asked if I would mind if he sent the X-ray to a physician friend. I agreed and, a week later, I was called into the coach's office. His physician friend had told him that this was a benign condition that should permit the young man to return to athletics. This created a difficult situation. I deemed it most important that this be recognized as an injury requiring the right management to prevent serious consequences that might otherwise result. Coach considered his friend's opinion to mean that the man could return to sports immediately.

To counter this, I sent copies of the X-rays to a number of orthopaedic surgeons across the country who were known for their special interests in cervical spinal injuries. I received prompt responses from eight of them agreeing with me, two were ambiguous. I presented my information to Dan and the matter was concluded. The player's neck was protected with a brace while the injury healed. He did return to playing football later.

The coach and I had a good relationship despite the above. I believe I had proven myself in one way or another. I found him to be rather philosophical at times when I had bad news about some player, especially if the man was one of those on whom he counted most. More than once, his response was: "We'll just have to dig a little deeper and come up with someone to do the job." Ara had said the same on at least one occasion.

As a coach, Dan knew the game and how to work with the assistant coaches under him. They seemed to do most of the actual coaching, conducting the practice sessions, and calling the plays. Dan did know what was going on and was on top of it. When it came to recruiting, he worked at it and did his part well. The academic requirements were a bother to him.

He also fared well in the record book at Notre Dame. He took the reins in 1976, won the "Gator Bowl" in 1976, and the Cotton Bowls in 1977 and 1978. He won the National Championship in 1977 with an 11-1 record.

I remember that one loss in 1977 better than many other games. We played Mississippi on September 17th down there. It was hotter than hell. It had to be over 100 degrees. No one offered to arrange for cooling fans. Even Gatorade could have been of some help to combat electrolyte losses through sweat that day, but Gatorade had not yet been developed. The best we could do was to give one salt tablet apiece to the players and push fluids on them. We tried to cool them by throwing wet towels over the guys' heads as they came off the field, exhausted, hot, and sweaty. Our ice ran out. Cold water for cooling and drinking was all we had. We learned that the Mississippi team had plenty of cokes for its players. We would have loved some of that.

Those of us on the sidelines all pitched in, working hard to help the players combat the heat. We had our own trainer, Gene Paszkiet, and several student trainers and managers to help look after the players. I myself was kept busy the same way. We wet towels, wrung them out partially in cool water. We then threw them around the men's heads and necks to cool them as they came from field to bench. One bucket of water turned red as Joe Restic came off the field with a bloody nose, dripping blood all the way. No fracture, but plenty of the red stuff anyway. The bleeding was soon controlled and shortly he was back in the game. Despite our best efforts in the heat, we lost that game 13-20.

After the game, a cooling shower and plenty of drinking water took care of things. I don't see how we managed to avoid more serious heat illness with so little to work with, but we did. It was not until we were on the bus on the way to the airport that heat illness showed up. Our quarterback, "Rusty Lisch" had a spell of weakness, a cold sweat, and nausea. It was obvious that he was about to vomit. We stopped the bus. I got off with him. He puked, a lot (all fluid), and then it was over—face wiped, mouth rinsed, back on the bus; more fluids, and then he was okay.

It surely would have been nice if someone had sent a case of coke over to us that day. There was no "Southern hospitality." State had a good opportunity to live up to that Southern reputation, but they blew it—and it wasn't the only time we missed out on Southern hospitality. Not only they, but also many parts of the country react the same way to the visiting teams, or to strangers.

Penn State fans seem to carry a chip on their shoulders. We found it necessary to elbow our way through the crowd in the stadium to get to the locker room at halftime. No simple passage—tough guys—they're glad to obstruct you and annoy you.

Michigan has the reputation for having a rowdy crowd of fans—drinking, cursing, abusive, and foul-mouthed. It is said to be closer to being an Ivy League school than any other in the Midwest—though surely not on such weekends (but I'm sure the reprobates are not of the student body either).

Southern Cal fans are a little rough on us, but in general, the West, the Midwest, Far West, Northwest, and Southwest are okay—and the East too. That leaves the Southeast and the South. They are the worst: drinking, shouting obscenities, foul-mouthed, disrespectful, obstreperous, and boisterous—not all schools, and not everyone, but just enough to give you a bad impression. The inhospitable rather hostile reactions by some fans certainly do not represent the school in most cases. Some fans are just "bad apples" in that way.

It is nothing to be taunted from the stands at any game, but to have half-filled cans of coke dumped and thrown at you (as at a game with Georgia Tech in Atlanta) deplores their sportsmanship, on which all sports are said to be built.

Even a school as fine as Clemson, with its great Southern traditions, had its face muddied when unruly fans spit upon us as we entered the small tunnel to exit the field after a game.

Worst of all was the occasion in 1978 when we had dead fish and empty whiskey bottles thrown at us at close range at the game with Georgia Tech. Things were so bad at that game (played at the Bobby Dodd Field in Atlanta, Georgia) that Coach Devine wisely stopped the game after one of our players turned and rushed to the first row of the stands to retaliate for the dangerous and insulting behavior to which we "mackerel snapper" Catholics were exposed. Dan then called us off the benches, which were close to the adjacent stands, and had all of us go out toward the middle of the field to escape the bottles and fish being thrown at us. Order was restored, but not the good feelings that should have prevailed. We won that game, 38 to 21.

NATIONAL CHAMPIONS
1977

Dan won his National Championship in 1977, in spite of that loss to Mississippi earlier in the year. We won the final game 38 to 10 on January 2, 1978, in the Cotton Bowl at Dallas. We went into that game with only a remote chance of winning the National Championship. I would say we rather "backed into it."

At the end of the regular season, we were ranked fifth and then we beat Texas (who had been ranked number one) in the Cotton Bowl. Oklahoma was ranked second and was favored by 13

"We're number one!"

points over number six Arkansas in their Bowl Game. It seemed that Arkansas would surely lose their game when their coach, Lou Holtz, sent his two best players—a runner and a pass receiver—

home for disciplinary reasons; however, Arkansas won, displacing Oklahoma who had been next in line for first place. Number three Alabama defeated Ohio State and looked to be National Champion if Texas were to lose. Number four Michigan lost to Washington. When Arkansas defeated Oklahoma who had been favored, Notre Dame won and rose to the top. The Irish were voted National Champion by a substantial margin, a blow to Alabama's hopes. And so we had jumped from fifth to first—with a lot of help form several teams who had been considered underdogs in their bowl games. And that's how we went from fifth to first place!

Devine had brought fame again to Notre Dame, but the University was not pleased with his personal approach to recruiting and goals. He knew good players and how to get them, but their morals and academics did not always meet Notre Dame's strict standards. According to the "underground," the school had made a few exceptions to accommodate the coach. Such actions eventually came between them, and his contract was allowed to expire.

The selection of the new coach was again a silent procedure. There were no rumors, no suggestion of who it was to be, just the timely announcement that another highly successful high school coach was to be the coach at Notre Dame: Gerry Faust.

Coach Gerry Faust
1981-1985

COACH FAUST had coached at Moeller High School in Cincinnati for eighteen years. He held an enviable record of 174 wins, 27 losses, and 2 ties. He had a great desire to succeed at Notre Dame, to join the ranks of Rockne and the other great coaches who had

Gerry Faust, highly successful high school coach is selected to be the next Head Football Coach at Notre Dame.

held forth at the school of Our Lady. The Coach had a very outgoing personality; he exuded a spirit of geniality and good will. It should have been easy to work with him and, in general, it was. He was a very religious man, but he was also not without his faults.

When he came to Notre Dame, we were forewarned that he used a number of doctors to look after his injured players at Moeller. That pattern gave the family practitioners the opportunity to maintain their personal doctor-patient relationship. That was undoubtedly a proper way to maintain continuity of care of their patients in high school sports. However, it also had the possibility of diluting the quality of care, since this might not have been the best choice of a doctor for a particular condition. At the college level, it could easily result in too many cooks in the kitchen. At Notre Dame, the responsibility was ours, and so at the first suggestion that the coach was going to bring outsiders into our circle, we (the medical team) reacted promptly to stop this action. It was our job to take care of these young men, and we would call for help when we needed it.

Coach Faust was a very religious man. His faith in God was manifested in many ways and times. He was a fine Catholic gentleman and such actions were indeed laudable. He relied heavily on prayer. The value of prayer in some of these situations interested me. We have all seen athletes in various sports who make the "sign of the cross," ostensibly asking for the Lord's help, or in some other way acknowledge such help. So many times have we turned to God for His help, even when we know we have not tried very hard to be in His good graces. In spite of that, we have no compunction in asking Him to take things in hand and shower us with His blessings, to turn the tables in our favor.

Coach Faust asked a lot of God to counter acts of fate. This was brought to my attention on an occasion when I was standing on the sidelines with Father Riehle, the team chaplain. ND had been working the ball down the field toward the south goal, but had stalled at about the twenty-yard line. It was fourth down as they lined up for a field goal. Gerry Faust, good man that he was, thought to beseech God for His help in this critical situation.

I recall Coach Faust striding quickly past us on the sideline. As Jerry came racing by, he turned for a moment and said quickly, "Say a Hail Mary, Doc. Say a Hail Mary, Father."

Father Riehle turned to me and said, "God doesn't have time for football. He has more important things to do." I agreed, but I also had some other thoughts on that subject, then as well as at other times.

Prayer

I AGREED THAT there were limits to the power of prayer under certain circumstances. For example, which team would have God's blessings when we play some other Christian college, with its players saying the same prayers we do?

My first thought was that prayer in such situations could indeed be helpful if the team was well prepared and had talent enough, and if God were standing around, waiting for our call. It can give you a sense of confidence—that you have all your bases covered with Him on your side. Actually, we believe it doesn't hurt to offer these prayers; things may be slow up there and you just might be heard.

His benevolence is also frequently sought from the very moment of an injury—especially by the parents—praying that their son, lying injured on the field, is not seriously hurt. The player has probably also called for divine help. Then there are the fans, medical staff, coaches and fellow players—many of them have already had their quick prayerful thoughts. Prayer promotes a sense of one's fate being in His hands and, if it is His will, so be it. It encourages a hopeful attitude and helps buoy the spirit that is floundering. Prayer throughout the entire period following the injury is also of value when combined with good medical care and hard work by the patient in his rehab process, but don't expect Him to do it alone. You have to do your share of the job.

Father Jim Riehle, team chaplain, a down-to-earth character and everyman's priest.

Finally, we do not deny God's presence. He is indeed there, guiding our judgment and providing us with the abilities to perform His work in surgery and with medicines—through our hands if necessary. He will find time to do that, whether for football players or not; but He doesn't seem to waste His time making field goals and touchdowns and, at Notre Dame, this is true despite the presence of "Touchdown Jesus," the mosaic emblazoned on the facing wall of the Hesburgh Library, opposite the north end of Notre Dame stadium. There He can be in close touch with events, in case He is really needed...and if He is not too busy.

The mosaic on the south wall of the Hesburgh Library, facing the Notre Dame Stadium, is known to the student body as "Touchdown Jesus."

I recalled the case of Larry Coutre in that game with Michigan State when I feared that he had suffered a serious injury to his neck as he came down headfirst. It was fortunate in the case of Larry Coutre, and other players who come down on their heads, endangering their necks, that serious injury does not occur. Our greatest fear at those moments is that the player could have suffered a neck injury that could result in paralysis. It was at those times that we tested God's powers with our prayers, and God answered. The athlete's training, conditioning, flexibility, and strengthening programs were also helpful in the prevention of an injury that could have been a very serious one.

But if Larry had suffered the severe injury that results in paralysis from the neck down, would that mean that God had been busy with other things that day? Moreover, if Larry recovered function, would that be God's doing? It certainly could be. He may have ordained that the paralysis was a mistake. He had an "ace in the hole." He would make this injury one of those from which one can recover.

Success

WE ENJOYED GOOD RELATIONSHIPS with Coach Faust. He was really a gentle and well-meaning man, of high moral character, and he was a good coach. He wanted so badly to succeed at Notre Dame, and we did too. And he was successful. He took his team to the 1983 Liberty Bowl and won, and the 1984 Aloha Bowl and won. However, his overall record of 30-26-1 did not satisfy the alumni, and so he was released after the 1985 season. He did not reach the pinnacle he had hoped for.

He loved the school and everything about it, and he still does. It is not unusual to see him at a Notre Dame home game even now, waving to his fans as he makes his way through the stadium. My work with the teams at Notre Dame ended in the spring of 1985. Gerry was to stay another year before the alumni had their way.

The Bowl Games

THE BOWL GAMES were like the proverbial "Pot of Gold," not only in the amount of money they generated for the athletic programs of the competing teams, but also as the "payoff" for a season of hard work for the players and staff. There was still work to be done in preparation for the game, and for the rigors of competition to be met by the ball players; but even to them, it was somewhat of a vacation—and to the staff, it was even more so. The staff included coaches, trainers, managers, doctors, all the front-office staff of secretaries, select ticket-office and business-office personnel, property man, and communications specialists, among others. Separate—and just as important—there was the entire band, and the cheerleaders.

Notre Dame had followed a policy of no post-season games for many years. The school had last played in a bowl game in 1925. They won that Rose Bowl game against Stanford, by a score of 27 to 10.

These games were often the season-ending game, determining the National Champion. Notre Dame was not about to allow itself to miss such an opportunity. After due consideration of these developments, and with pragmatic consideration of the financial rewards of such participation, ND gave in to their second thoughts about bowl games and decided it was time to have a "go" at it again. The Bowls were glad to include them since Notre Dame was always a big attraction. And ND was glad to oblige.

The Bowls themselves were gigantic promotions. Good teams, good competition, good football, and the outstanding athleticism of the players provided a grand show worthy of the advanced ticket prices of these competitions. The Bowl committees met with wide civic approval and collaboration. Promotional dinners and celebrations were the order of the day. A bowl queen and her retinue were selected. Showmanship abounded. The teams and all associated with the effort were welcomed and recognized for their attainment of the lofty assignment to that game. Each of these Bowl committees and communities worked hard to ensure the success of their Bowl Game, which would bring prestige and profit to their city. Each Bowl had its own personality that was extended by its promoters and hospitality committees.

The Cotton Bowl Games
1970, 1971

OUR FIRST TWO Bowl Games were in the Cotton Bowl against the University of Texas. We were heartily welcomed by the community and its committees. The hospitality of the Southwest is underrated.

The Texans chose to hang on to their "Howdy, Podner" image, taking the group to a cowboy-town movie lot one afternoon and giving the team a try at calf wrestling on another occasion. Western-style barbecues competed for popularity with elite dining in the evening. This was a real bonanza for the team and the staff. The labors of all were paying off big.

The first of these games was on January 1, 1970. Texas was the #1 team that year. Darryl Royal had developed a strong team that had established its superiority with an offense based on the wishbone. This was a relatively new concept and Texas used it to their advantage. ND lost that Bowl Game 21-17 to the #1 team, but only for that year.

ND went back to the 1971 Cotton Bowl the following year and again played Texas, who was ranked #2 at that time. Ara, his offensive coordinator, Tom Pagna, and his defensive coaches, Paul Shoults, George Kelly, and Joe Yonto, had devised a "mirror defense" which was highly successful in stopping Texas, 24-11. ND became the team ranked second to Nebraska, who had been ranked number one.

I was with the team for these games, except the first Bowl Game. Dr. Howard Engel was one of the physicians assisting in the care of ND athletes at that time. One of our very good quarterbacks, Coley O'Brien, was a diabetic who had to be monitored carefully during stressful activities such as this Bowl Game. It was Howard's duty as our internist to keep Coley fit. With his diabetes controlled, Coley played in the game and performed capably. This was pay-off time for Howard too.

We were fortunate both of these years in not having any serious injuries. Texas is always a tough, hard-nosed team but so were we. This was a matter of two clean, hard-hitting and well-conditioned teams playing hard and by the rules. Under those circumstances, injuries are less likely to occur than in games in which flagrant violations of sportsmanship are seen.

The Orange Bowl
1972

IN 1972, NOTRE DAME had a shot at Nebraska, who had won the Orange Bowl the two preceding years. They were a good team but had already lost two games and tied one, so they could be taken. Our team trained hard. It would not be an easy game. Nebraska was tough and just as big as we were, and they did have an outstanding player, Johnny Rodgers, who could cause a lot of trouble as a runner, passer, and pass receiver. His reputation was good enough to keep us from developing a false sense of security.

We went down to Miami and spent almost a week there, completing our training and preparing for the game, while also enjoying the high-cost ambience of our beach hotel. The local committees served us well, providing the team and staff with parties and dining to make it outstanding in that respect.

The game was played the evening of January 1, 1973. It didn't take long to sense the outcome. Johnny Rodgers was just too much for us. His coach kindly pulled him in the third quarter. He had done enough. This had to have been one of the best one-man performances on record against Notre Dame. Rodgers scored every possible way—running, passing, and receiving. Nebraska won 40 to 6. Notre Dame was ranked no better than 14th nationally that year.

The Sugar Bowl
1973

THIS YEAR FOUND US in New Orleans, enjoying the cosmopolitan atmosphere of the city. The Sugar Bowl committees showed us how hospitable the South could be, welcoming us with the good food and entertainment for which it is famous. They did well for the team and treated our staff contingent with dinners at their best restaurants, such as Antoine's and Captain Alexander's. The players were also appropriately feted and had the opportunity to meet some Southern Belles as well. It doesn't get any better than that.

The game was played on December 31, 1973. ND defeated

#1 Alabama, 24-23, in the Sugar Bowl in a game with a dramatic finish. In the course of a tight game, Notre Dame had just pulled ahead of Alabama with a field goal which made the score 24-23 in favor of the Irish, with a little over four minutes to play. We had to keep that lead, but shortly things were not going well. We were backed up to our two-yard line and it was now third and nine. Ara called time. He called the team to the sidelines and outlined a play.

Robin Weber

The referee blew his whistle. The time-out was over.

The teams lined up. Tom Clements was at quarterback. The ball was snapped. He appeared to hand off to our halfback, Eric Penick, who charged into the line. The Alabama defenders were drawn to Eric. Meanwhile, Tom faked a pass to Dave Casper, his favorite target running across the middle. As the safety came up to cover Casper, Clements caught sight of Robin Weber racing by the defender. Robin was not the man usually playing that end position. He was not a likely receiver. ND had thrown only one pass to him during the regular season. He was not the favorite target of Tom Clements, not the man you would expect to be the one to turn to at such a moment. Before the defender could recover, Clements lofted a pass to Robin who caught it and hung onto it as he was tackled.

It was a gain good enough to give us a first down and the opportunity to run down the clock. The game ended in our favor 24-23. ND became #1, the National Champion.

The Orange Bowl
1975

ON JANUARY 1, 1975, ND would again face Alabama—this time in the Orange Bowl game. The Crimson Tide was again the number one team in the country. We prepared for the game while staying at Marco Island. This was a real Florida vacation on the beach of a resort hotel. We spent Christmas there, allowing only a brief practice that day since a big Christmas dinner had been planned for the team and the staff. We didn't even miss the snow of a white Christmas. The team enjoyed the food, the water, and the resort activities. One of these activities, unfortunately, led to Greg Collins falling off a rented motorbike. He incurred a gash on the front of one of his knees. He was taken to the emergency room at the hospital in Naples. The wound was cleansed and sutured. Antibiotics were started and the worries began. Could he play? Greg was team co-captain and played capably as outside linebacker. We needed him.

Christmas came while we were preparing there for the game. All the players, regardless of their religious denomination, typically attended Mass with the staff before a game. Mass on Christmas Eve was one more such occasion.

Christmas Day meant a light workout day for the team but a day heavy with food. All in attendance were well sated during this holiday with turkey and all the trimmings. Then the serious side of the trip began.

We moved to Miami the next day, winding down the practice sessions. We were royally entertained by the Orange Bowl committee. These people were accustomed to grandiose ways. These sophisticates of Miami showed us a good time with an afternoon of boating, exploring the waters of the coastline, and providing for sumptuous dining for the staff and players on several occasions. A dinner party for the two teams and staffs after the game was held at an exclusive country club, with the best of food and mounds of shrimp for starters.

I inspected Greg Collin's knee daily. The wound was clean and healing well. On game day, there was some residual tenderness, so I injected the skin around the wound with a local anesthetic just before the game. He played well until another injury forced him to the sidelines. Healing of the knee wound was not disturbed.

His replacement was Marvin Russell. He was next to incur injury. He was seeing tough action as a linebacker when he suffered a compound dislocation of the proximal finger joint of the middle finger just before halftime. The wound was clean, no dirt or grass was ground into it. Under local anesthesia in the locker room, his hand was scrubbed and prepared for surgery. The wound was thoroughly cleansed and irrigated. The dislocation was reduced. It was stable. The wound was closed. The finger was splinted and a bulky dressing was applied. Antibiotics were started. Marvin played the second half well. The finger was splinted for ten days thereafter. It was inspected daily for any suggestion of infection that might require further care of the injury. The finger healed uneventfully.

Gene Paszkiet, our trainer, taught me a lesson at halftime in that Orange Bowl against Alabama: Always check the field before you leave it to see that all your players are off the field and that they are okay. The first half had ended and all of us headed for the locker room. I usually went off the field with Gene but I didn't see him in our group. Then I saw him, on the other side of the field, supporting one of our players who was painfully holding his arm as they walked cautiously off the field. I had not realized we were about to leave an injured player behind as we walked to the locker room.

The appearance of the injured player's elbow was typical. I had seen enough dislocated elbows to recognize this one. In the locker room, I further examined the man and found no suggestion of fracture. We had local anesthetics with us, so I reduced the dislocation under local anesthesia. With one of the student trainers providing counter-traction at the area of the shoulder, and a manager providing steady traction to the arm while I maintained the elbow in slight flexion, I manipulated the elbow and reduced the dislocation. Reduction was almost painless, to the great relief of the player. The joint was stable. A sling maintained the corrected position of the elbow. A posterior plaster splint was applied the next day. The eventual outcome was good.

The game itself was a close game with a good Alabama team. The final score was 13-11 in our favor. Alabama lost its 1st place standing, falling to 5th, while ND went from 8th to 6th place after that game.

The Gator Bowl
1976

JACKSONVILLE WAS HOME to the Gator Bowl. They had not yet achieved the status of the other major Bowls, but they did a good job at trying to catch up to the larger and more established top-tier Bowls. They saw to it that we enjoyed their hospitality—big dinners, side trips to Sea World, and just walking the beach.

We had our practice sessions at a nearby school and then a final workout was planned for the evening before the game. I remember going to the practice that evening, which was to be just a light workout in the stadium in which we would play. The team had already started their drills when I arrived. The trainers met me with one of our players, Ted Horansky, who was coming off the field clutching his hand. He had suffered a compound dislocation of the thumb at the metacarpo-phalangeal joint, by which the thumb joins the hand. This had occurred in the course of the routine warm-up. We found a driver and vehicle that took us to the hospital. There, I persuaded the E.R. personnel to allow me to do the work on my man under a local anesthetic. Ted was given a nerve block. Again, the wound was a clean one, no dirt or grass in it. The wound was cleansed, and copiously irrigated. The dislocation was reduced. The capsule and skin were closed since I was available to check on him daily. A cast was applied. Antibiotic therapy was started. Ted did not play in that game. Healing was uneventful.

We played Penn State on December 26 of 1976 in the Gator Bowl and won 20-9, a victory that elevated ND from 20th to 12th in the national rankings.

The Cotton Bowl
1977-78

THE 1977 COTTON BOWL brought us back to Texas. Again, we were up against the number one team in the nation. We anticipated another shootout, which only the best man would win. Texas was undefeated. Much of the credit for those wins belonged to Earl Campbell, Texas' star running back who was big, strong, and fast. But Notre Dame was confident. They were having a good season and saw no reason for that to change.

On January 2, 1978, ND took the #1 ranking away from Texas again and made it their own with a 38-10 win in the 1977 Cotton Bowl. Notre Dame was declared the National Champion after that game.

Notre Dame was back in the 1978 Cotton Bowl for a game against a good team from the University of Houston.

The game was played on January 1, 1979, in what has become known as the "Ice Bowl." Joe Montana firmly solidified his reputation here as "the comeback kid" under freezing weather conditions, with a legendary game and performance. ND finished 6th in the UPI rankings that year.

That game is worthy of special note. It ranks with other legendary games in Notre Dame history. It will be discussed later as one of the legends of Notre Dame.

The Mirage Bowl
1979

WHEN WE WENT TO JAPAN to play in the Nissan "Mirage Bowl" in Tokyo in 1979, the contract expressly insisted that the entire band and cheerleaders were to be part of the Notre Dame contingent. The Japanese wanted the whole show, and they got it—and enjoyed it.

We were there for about a week, training and then playing the game. Meanwhile we were shown real Oriental hospitality. Cars were at our disposal; young college people were assigned to assist our group in any arrangements we needed—shopping for clothing, cameras, and more. We visited the Emperor's Palace, the Ginza (Tokyo's Times Square), their flea market, and the business district. We took the "bullet train" to Kyoto to visit their National Shrine. Their young people, our escorts, did very well with the English language. Our personal escort, who was really assigned to assist Coach Devine, was a lovely, personable young lady named, of all things, "O'Hara." That sounded strange to us because she obviously was not Irish, but it apparently is a well-known Japanese name, pronounced differently, with an "ah" for the letter "a." She was constantly available to help us. We hated to leave her when the time came, and she too seemed genuinely distressed. When we left, she gave each of us a very small gift, as was their custom—an ornamental fan. Her assistance and that of the other young people helped make our stay easy and enjoyable.

The players were entertained with big parties; they also managed to get around town to see some of the sights. We were impressed with modern Japan—its cleanliness, its efficiency, and the huge population all busily engaged in commerce and living their daily lives amidst such crowding.

The Japanese saw to it that we were entertained well. They had arranged for a very ostentatious party, not only for the dignitaries and staffs associated with the Miami and Notre Dame teams, but also for all the higher Nissan executives and supporters of the Mirage Bowl. This Bowl was promoted by the Nissan Company, automobile manufacturers. It was a grand affair. Everyone learned to eat sushi at that lavish party, with lots of other good, delicious, and strange foods. For our further entertainment, they presented an ensemble of drummers from Northern Japan attired only in loincloths, who rotated through a fast-moving, tightly timed display of precision drumming. They played a wide variety of percussion instruments, to the appreciation and admiration of all present.

The Mirage Bowl was a once-in-a-lifetime experience. We were fortunate to have been part of that occasion. It was a treat for the staff, and even more, it was a cultural experience for the team and for us. The Japanese obviously enjoyed the game. Their thing was to wave pom-poms during the entire game to show their support, which they did, and they waved tens of thousands of them. It was a colorful sight. It was impossible to determine the team they favored because they waved for everyone and everything, every play—just as it should be. Then, as soon as the game ended, the athletes walked and jogged around the track surrounding the gridiron, as was their custom, to more applause, cheering, and waving of pom-poms. Our team was happy to do so.

The final score was Notre Dame 40, Miami 15.

It was not one of the Bowl Games winding up the football season, not one that determined national rankings, other than by entering the won-loss records of the competing teams. The "real" Bowl Games were post seasonal, invitational contests. The Mirage Bowl was the final game on the regular schedule for ND and Miami, with the game having been moved to Tokyo by mutual agreement.

The Sugar Bowl
1980

HERE WE WERE, back in New Orleans. This time we would play in the new indoor bowl. We again had a shot at the number one team in the nation, Georgia. We would play them on January 1, 1981. The Sugar Bowl people were as genial and hospitable as they could be with the usual parties, scrumptious food, and entertainment.

However, it didn't take long once the game started to get that sweet taste out of our mouths. Things didn't go as well as the final score suggested—a seven-point difference. There were at least two plays that made a big difference in the game.

The first was to have Georgia kick to us on the kickoff and watch our two halfbacks allow the ball to fall to the ground between them as a Georgia player raced down the field and pounced on the ball, giving it to them near our goal line. They had a quick and easy score there. The second was an injury to the hand of our quarterback, Mike Courey. I took him to the Emergency Room at Tulane University where X-rays revealed a fracture of one of the central metacarpal bones. I reduced the fracture under local anesthesia and applied a cast, but he was done for the game.

ND lost to Georgia 17-10, enabling Georgia to keep their #1 ranking. ND was 9th in the final AP ratings.

The Liberty Bowl
1983

MY LAST BOWL GAME was on December 29, 1983, in the Liberty Bowl. There was good entertainment to be had there. The music on Beale Street equaled the best. The Liberty Bowl people arranged an exhibition of clog dancing for us, and provided for a private River Boat excursion with music and dancing one evening. My daughter Beth was with me. My wife Bunny was not with us. She was home completing arrangements for the wedding of our son, Michael, who was to marry a nice South Bend girl, Carol

Lowe, a day or so after we returned. Beth and Coach Brian Boulac stole the show that evening with their jitterbug dancing. The game was another frigid experience. A night game played in freezing weather. ND won a thrilling 19-18 victory over Boston College. Although Doug Flutey was their quarterback, he did not complete his "Hail Mary Pass" this time. ND was ranked 18th in the season final New York Times computer rankings.

The Notre Dame Family

IT WAS A DISTINCT PLEASURE to be associated with the team on these trips. Everything had been arranged for the entire assemblage. Bus to the airport. Get on the plane. Get off to the cheers of loyal alumni, the band playing the ND Fight Song as you land and deplane and at your destination. Bus to the hotel where another welcoming band and group of fans are waiting. At the hotel, get your room key and assignments. Get your per diem at the desk. Then pick up the schedule for meetings, Mass, and meals.

All of us pretty much became one big family. That happens when you and the other members of your group are displaced among mostly strangers. Our primitive instincts, our herd mentality, bound us to our others, seeking comfort with them. We worked together, and we relaxed and played together. We ate with our group, and we partied with our group. There was the unspoken sense that we were all in this together, and we were. We were also conscious of our duties, obligations, and responsibilities. The hosts at each of the Bowls had planned extensive parties, dinners, and entertainment, but we did not forget that we came to play with hopes of winning. That meant practice sessions for the team.

Gene Paszkiet, our trainer, was ill and did not come with us to these last Bowl Games. He had developed a malignant lymphoma, a condition that was ultimately fatal. His football and working days were over. I would lose this good friend in a few months.

He pointed out to us, when he stuck his head in the door of the bus for the last time as the team was about to leave Notre Dame for the airport: "Okay, you guys. When you get down there, don't forget what Mark Anthony said to Cleopatra when he went to see her in Egypt. 'I didn't come here to hold hands.' Don't forget it. You've got business to attend to."

Domer Sports Heroes and Legends

IT IS NOT ONLY IN FOOTBALL that we have these sports heroes They come in all sizes, colors, and degrees in the various athletic endeavors into which they channel their energies. It's just that the possibility of becoming heroic is greater in football and the other contact sports than in less violent activities. In some cases, I would consider it brave or heroic simply to expose oneself to such violence and danger.

Reggie Ho, diminutive kicker, was never injured but he exposed his small frame to the onrushing giant linemen time and again, concentrating on the kick rather than self-protection.

And how about those plucky hockey players eager to get back into the melee as soon as I finished suturing their lacerations!

Then there were the guys who had undergone knee, shoulder, back and other surgical procedures who labored to regain their spot on the team despite the risk of re-injury.

They received no gold medals or any other recognition as a rule. They appeared to be simply doing their duty. I saw it many times to be above and beyond one's duty. They do not consider it heroic although they demonstrate the spirit and "heart" of heroes. They just want so badly to get back into the lineup. They are willing to take their chances. They labor and play not for themselves alone; they play for their fellow players, their team, and the duty to win. They will themselves to face the rigors and dangers of rugged competition that places them into a special class of men. They give of themselves for this. Are these not heroes?

The Legend of Joe Montana

AT ANY TIME that there is talk of heroes at Notre Dame, the oft-repeated names of its legendary characters will surface—for example, the name of Joe Montana. He proved himself on numerous occasions to be "the comeback kid" with his performances as field general and passing "Ace" as seen here early in the 1977 season. And at that, he could be no better than he proved himself to be in the 1978 Cotton Bowl game in Dallas.

This became one of the legendary stories in Notre Dame history—the Joe Montana "Chicken Soup" story, also known as the game played in the "Ice Bowl." It was actually in the 1978 Cotton Bowl game in Dallas on January 1 of 1979 against the University of Houston. The story has been told many times by various authors, with each rendition being just a bit different from the others, but I would like to tell it to you as it actually occurred. I was there.

Of the various versions of the story that you will hear and read, there is one version which I found in a children's book that comes closer to being accurate than any other in the telling of this legendary game. It was written by Joe Unis. He too should know the story well because he was there too. Joe Unis was our place kicker.

Joe Unis has not received the credit he deserves for his role in that legend. He was not our regular place kicker. Chuck Male, our kicker, was injured and did not play in that game. Joe doesn't

Joe Montana's passing, running, and field leadership in 1977 confirmed him as "the comeback kid."

usually have his name mentioned until near the end of the story. But what a finish! What performance under pressure! And the need to repeat his performance staggers the imagination! If it were not for him, there would be no legend. So perhaps the legend should be the Joe Unis-Joe Montana story.

On the other hand, if Kris Haines had not hung onto Montana's passes, there would be no legend. In fact, we had better include every man on that field in the legend. If any one of them had failed in his assignment in those last few plays in Dallas, there would be no story. However, since it would be too unwieldy to name all these men in the title of this event, let us continue to refer to it as "The Joe Montana Chicken Soup Story." It is the story of that game in which he cemented his fame as "the comeback kid." And so, let us give Joe the great credit which is his due on that day of heroes, while we mentally acknowledge all the unsung heroes of that game, as so often occurs in every great moment in history.

There are really two beginnings to this story. They will converge to a dramatic finish. The story of the game and the events related to the "chicken soup" are the true story, just as it happened on that icy day in Dallas.

* * * * *

One bit of this history begins with Joe's personality, which for this moment we will simplify as being very independent. He knew his worth to the team, possibly even better than did the coach, but the players knew. That was the "scoop" behind the scenes. There were two other good quarterbacks rated above Joe. Although Joe was rated third string at that time, the players had the utmost confidence in Montana's abilities. The feeling was that he had that little something "extra." He instilled confidence in his teammates.

Joe's streak of willfulness put him at odds with the coach who demanded that certain rules and restrictions related to the training of a group of spirited young men be observed by all—without exception—even by exceptional players. The coach stood by his guns and so did Montana.

One tool in the disciplinary armamentarium that could be used by coaches with recalcitrant players was to demote them to an inferior status in the rankings, thereby limiting the playing time of that man. If the coach truly saw the man as less talented, inferior in any way, he could hardly be criticized for placing the man lower in rank for that position. But in this case, it was regarded as spiteful by many, including Joe's teammates, and especially those teammates who knew that Joe was a better quarterback than Coach Devine would acknowledge.

ND was fortunate to have a good stable of quarterbacks that year, 1978. They were all good, highly qualified, and well regarded, which made Devine's ranking of them reasonable. We have to accept the fact that a head coach at this level of competition has the ability to see those subtle differences in the player's ability to perform his skills by which he rates them as first, second, or third string. It was hard to argue with Dan's decisions at that point, early in the season. However, after that game with Purdue at Lafayette, Indiana, on September 30th, there was no longer room for argument.

Montana was a bench warmer when we arrived for the game at Purdue, third string quarterback, rankled, puzzled, but confident. Ahead of him were two other good and capable quarterbacks. Unfortunately, the team had lost the first two games of that season and was behind in scoring against Purdue when a critical point was reached in the game.

The team had looked forward to playing Purdue, one of Notre Dame's perennially bitter foes—the one who had broken ND's string of 39 consecutive unbeaten games in South Bend in 1950. ND always looked to avenge that defeat.

Game Day was a beautiful, warm day in the fall of that year. The trip down to Lafayette was colorful, the leaves having started to color the landscape with their hues of orange, red, and gold. The team was in good shape—no serious carry-over injuries to mar the effort. A strong team, loaded with talented, young players. Of course, you could say the same about Purdue. And both teams were playing on the same field under the same conditions. It is under such circumstances that being a little better here or a bit better at that makes the difference. Lady Luck often enters such conflicts as well. Prayer is not helpful in winning since both teams get God's attention if he has nothing better to do. We do have to look to Him, however, to protect both teams as well as He can. We do not wish injury or misfortune to befall either team.

Notre Dame, having said their prayers at Mass that morning and prayers before the game, was well prepared with prayers, good training, coaching, and conditioning. So was Purdue, although we may have had an edge in the prayer department. Luck could go either way. Leahy had a saying that "a team makes its own breaks." There had to be some further intangible that would decide that game.

The game began with Rusty Lisch as quarterback. He just wasn't as good that day as he could be against that opposition. As the game proceeded, Purdue was ahead 24-14. Our passing attack had not been going well against Purdue's defense. Lisch was replaced by Gary Forystek who did well until he went down with a neck injury. This was the kind of injury that is inherently critical. It was obviously of some severity, painful with even the slightest movement, muscles tight and in spasm, with the only encouraging sign being the normal function present in all extremities.

A neck brace was carefully applied. An ambulance was driven out onto the field. Gary was carefully placed on a stretcher, the helmet still on his head. (It was not removed to avoid moving his head and neck about.) Gary's head and helmet were taped to the stretcher to prevent movement of the injured part until X-rays could be taken. He was loaded into the ambulance.

Dr. Earl Heller, an associate of Dr. Denham's, was at the game. He came down on the field and was pressed into service. He accompanied Forystek to the hospital. X-rays there revealed an un-displaced fracture of the cervical spine, in good position. Dr. Heller accompanied Gary on the trip back to South Bend in the ambulance and arranged for Gary's hospitalization. Treatment would require protection of the fractured area of the spine with a cervical brace for two months. After a few days, Gary returned to school wearing the brace. Everything went well thereafter, but Gary did not return to football at Notre Dame. He did try out for the pros the following year but was unsuccessful. His career ended there.

Forystek was replaced by Rusty Lisch, but again, things just didn't click for him. In desperation, Coach Devine called on Montana to finish the game. Joe's life was to change.

Notre Dame was ten points behind Purdue when Joe went in, early in the fourth quarter of the game. It wasn't long before Dave Reeve kicked a field goal. Shortly thereafter, Luther Bradley intercepted a pass, giving us the ball. Montana came through with a touchdown pass to Ken MacAfee. That tied the score at 24-24.

We kicked off but Purdue soon returned the kick to us. We were on our 30-yard line when Joe completed a couple of passes to Kris Haines and the same to Ken MacAfee. Notre Dame now went to the ground game and two plays later, David Mitchell scored. Reeve's kick made the final score 31-24.

With this stellar performance, Joe was no longer a third-string quarterback. He became ND's first-string quarterback and was a "fixture" at that position when we went to Dallas for the Cotton Bowl at the end of the 1978 season.

* * * * *

The other half of this story begins with my own family. Beth, the youngest of our nine children and fourteen years of age at the time, was with my wife and me in Dallas for the 1979 Cotton Bowl Game. She and my wife were guests of the University. The families of the staff, coaches, and others associated with the team through the year were given this bonus of attending the bowl games.

We were housed in fine hotels, dined to haute cuisine, and were entertained each day in various ways to make it a well-deserved vacation, a "payback" to the team and staff for their good, season-long work for the program. We received an allowance, per diem, which Beth and the other kids spent readily. They then started making charges to the family credit card. Kids today are smart that way.

We all looked forward to playing Houston, a good team with a 9-2 record, as well as enjoying the party atmosphere that surrounded these Bowl Games. Our team went through its practices daily but they also participated in the special programs, parties, and dinners arranged for them. They were enjoying the fruits of their labors.

Now let's get back to Beth. At home, the routine on Christmas Eve found the kids hanging their stockings above the fireplace. They would awaken the next morning to find that Santa had visited overnight. This time, we sneaked a few things into Beth's room, which adjoined ours in the hotel, after she was asleep. But we were the ones to be surprised the next morning to find that Santa had made a second visit in the early hours of the morning, leaving my wife Bunny and me with stockings full of candy, gum, fruit, little toys, a packet of tea, and a packet of Mrs. Grass's Noodle

Soup. We regularly carried our coffee maker on such trips to brew coffee or tea in the morning. What a thoughtful thing for Bethie to give us the tea and noodle soup. It was a nice surprise, and how convenient it proved to be later.

Dallas was experiencing unusual weather conditions at this time. A cold rain had fallen the day before the game, and overnight the temperature fell well below freezing. It was a beautiful picture. The branches of the trees were encased in ice—beautiful, glistening, crystalline ice. Unfortunately, the weight of the ice caused the tree limbs to droop ominously and, in many cases, branches had broken and fallen, causing problems in some parts of the city where there were disruptions of telephone and electrical services, creating havoc in the midst of this beauty.

On the day preceding the game, a reception for the combined staffs of the two teams and the Cotton Bowl Committee was held at the large and beautiful suburban home of one of the supporters of the event. However, the party was short lived since the house was without heat for some time prior to the reception because of the storm. It wasn't very comfortable. We were glad to pay our respects and then return to our warm hotel.

On our return to the hotel, we had a hot cup of tea made with Beth's packet of tea in our convenient coffee pot. That pot surely did come in handy on many occasions when traveling. I never would have guessed that it was to become an item in ND history.

That night, the night before the big game, the team was taken to a secluded, quiet place—a seminary in this case—to avoid the distractions of the rowdy crowds in the hotel. This was the usual routine the night before a game. The team members needed their rest to be well prepared for the following day, which was New Year's Day, January 1, 1979, the day of the Cotton Bowl game between Notre Dame and the Houston Cougars.

After a good night's rest, the team had their breakfast at the seminary. They prepared to take their bus to the Cotton Bowl.

I waited at the hotel with my wife and Beth for the bus that would later take the official party to the game.

Our trainer, Gene Paszkiet, had called me earlier that morning to inform me that one of our big linemen was ill—stomach upset. He couldn't keep his food down all night, and would I bring out some soup or something bland that might stay with him. I went to the hotel kitchen but they had not yet prepared soup for the day. Then I recalled the packet of Mrs. Grass' Noodle Soup that Beth had given us, so I went to the stadium armed with that packet and our coffee maker to warm water for the soup.

The chartered bus picked us up. We arrived at the Cotton Bowl about a half hour before game time. It was a bitter cold, gray day and it would remain so for the entire game. Both Beth and my wife had good seats—fifty-yard line, sixth row. How can you complain about that? I believe you can, if there is no heat and the temperature throughout the game is freezing.

My wife and Beth found their seats in the stands caked in ice, as was the entire stadium. The weather guaranteed to make this a miserable experience from that point of view. My ladies had tried to dress well for the weather: heavy coats, sweaters, long pants with liners, boots, thick felt hats, mufflers, gloves, blankets, and very important, newspapers and cardboard for their seats and to be placed beneath their feet. It wasn't enough for comfort. The temperature throughout most of the game hovered around seventeen degrees Fahrenheit, with a wind-chill factor between zero and minus fifteen degrees. The game had been a "sellout" for weeks, but today the stands were barely more than half filled, and by the end of the game, only a scattering of fans remained in their seats. But my two ladies were no wimps. They were cold and miserable but they stayed to the end. Real fans. Real troopers.

When I arrived at the stadium, I left them and proceeded to the locker room. My job was there, with the team. When I arrived, the guys were getting dressed for the game. They had put on an extra layer to ward off the cold. I carried in my packet of soup mix and the coffee maker. Dr. Thompson, who was the University physician at this time, was with me. Gene Paszkiet, the head trainer, met us with a somewhat relieved attitude when we entered the locker room. He informed me that happily, the soup would not be needed. The player had recovered and had managed to eat a decent breakfast. I put my stuff on the windowsill in the trainer's room.

The players, trainers, and coaches finished dressing, taping, and going through their usual preparations before a game. At a signal from the field, the guys pulled themselves together, gathering around the door, waiting for the signal to leave.

The team was ready. They shuffled out into the cold, through the tunnel and out to the field. These activities were all planned to the minute. Players left the room at designated intervals for each of the groups of men, spending so many minutes on the field going through certain warm-up routines, one eye on the clock, and at a signal, they returned to the locker room. Everything went by schedule.

I went out too. It was cold! The field of synthetic turf had been covered, giving us a dry, cold, and hard field on which to play the game. I retreated to the locker room as soon as I felt familiar with the surroundings and after meeting the doctor and trainers of the Houston team. We determined the availability of whatever help we might need, including the availability and location of the ambulance.

Back in the locker room shortly before game time, some players needed a little more taping; they used the lavatory once more; they snugged up their equipment, and for a short while, they just sat around, anxiously awaiting the start of the game. Some chatted a bit. A couple of coaches had last-minute suggestions for individual players who were already in a light sweat from their exertion, in spite of the weather. The temperature was still seventeen degrees. The wind-chill factor was somewhere below zero. That sweat already on their bodies would make the cold even worse on those who were not in the active lineup when they returned to the field. They mentioned the cold, but did not complain. It "went with the territory." They came to play. No complaining about the weather.

The fellows tried to relax for a short time, resting on the blanketed floor or at ease, sitting before their lockers. There wasn't much conversation. Some went through one or another type of mental psyching of themselves for the battle ahead. A last-minute admonition or instruction from their position coaches completed the preparations.

At a signal from the field, the team prepared to leave the locker room. Coach Devine gathered the men around him, and gave them a few brief words, which were meant to be inspirational. He then turned to Father Riehle who led the team in prayer. Then with a shout of "Okay! Let's go!" they left the warmth of that room for the cold, bleak, wintry battlefield on which they would wage their fight for the next several hours in the bitter cold.

They went out and massed in the tunnel and areaway to wait for a signal, at which they rushed out on the field with the band blaring and cheerleaders running ahead in their blue and gold Notre Dame outfits, but today in more embellished outfits than usual, with layers of hosiery, body shirts, heavy underwear and stocking hats. A shout went up from the crowd as the entire troupe ran onto the field. I thought the cheer was a little weak for an ND crowd. Maybe the ski masks covering the faces and mouths of the spectators muffled their cheers. The team took a quick warm-up run and a brief workout on the field.

My daughter Beth and my wife and many of the families of our staff were in the stands, sitting there on papers and cardboard to insulate them from the ice-coated seats. There were many "no-shows" for that game, and many fans who gave up to the cold.

The game soon started. The Houston Cougars were a rugged team. They were the champions of the Southwest Conference and, although Notre Dame was ahead 12-0 at the end of the first quarter, the Cougars were ahead 20-12 at halftime. The scoring had gone back and forth, and Notre Dame was behind. Montana was not having a good day thus far.

The weather was formidable. The temperature was barely tolerable with a twenty-five mile an hour gusting wind whipping the seventeen-degree weather into a biting, bitter cold. Those playing worked up a sweat in a hurry, despite the cold; such were their efforts in the game. They came off the field as defenses and offenses changed places, cold on the outside, their internal heat shown by their hot breaths blowing steam as they sought cover from the cold. We threw their field coats over them as they came off. These were lightweight, all-purpose jackets of a material more like canvas than anything else. These coats were only lightly lined, and not very warm. They served to contain a player's body heat and to give protection from the wind. They were not great for these conditions, but that was all we had. They were at a premium. We tried to get them to the fellows actively playing, as they came off the field. I managed to hide from the cold in one of them from time to time. I was shivering with the cold by halftime.

And so was Joe Montana. He had been playing with short

sleeves, bare armed below the elbow, the only one on the field so dressed. He wanted nothing to interfere with his throwing the ball. With this additional exposure of his body, his heat loss was excessive. When he came off the field, he was shivering uncontrollably. He was hypothermic with a temperature of 96 degrees. We got him on the trainer's table and piled what coats and blankets were available over him. It was then that I spotted my coffee maker.

Just what we needed for hot soup!

In short order, we had hot water and, after adding the contents of the packet of Mrs. Grass' Noodle Soup mix, we got some hot soup into Joe, who gradually responded. His temperature was still below normal when the team returned to the field. Dr. Thompson stayed in the locker room with Montana until Joe felt well and had stopped shivering. His temperature returned to normal.

We were still in the third quarter when Dr. Thompson brought Joe out. The guys were not into shouting "Hallelujah" or they would have done so when they saw Joe.

Things were not going well on the field. Tim Koegel, our back-up quarterback, was capable at his job, but he was not having a good day. The scoreboard had us twenty-two points behind in the third quarter. The score was 34-12 in favor of Houston. Joe was on the sidelines with us, trying to keep warm in one of those flimsy coats. Gene Paszkiet had told the coach that Joe was ready. At a signal from the coach, Montana threw off the jacket and began to throw a few passes on the sideline. He ran a few short sprints behind the benches, and then pronounced himself ready to go. Gene Paszkiet, Dr. Green, Dr. Thompson, and I all eagerly agreed that Joe was ready, and we knew that he was needed.

With Joe back in the game, the team's hopes surged. The score was still 34-12 when Joe went in. Time remaining in the third quarter was four minutes and forty seconds, with Notre Dame behind. There was a sense of confidence that emanated from Joe, one of his trademarks, which was transmitted to the team. They continued to feel even more that they had a chance to win with him back in the game.

He was not an immediate hero. He threw an interception and completed only one pass out of eleven in the third quarter. Then he started the fourth quarter by throwing an interception. Things were still not going well. This was our would-be hero performing this way? We just weren't getting anywhere—but wait! With the clock showing 7:37 of the fourth quarter left to be played, Houston had the ball for a series and, at this point, they failed as they tried to make a first down. They prepared to kick. The ball was centered to their punter, and as he kicked the ball, it was blocked by Tony Belden. Steve Cichy alertly and promptly picked up the ball and ran 33 yards for a touchdown. Wow! Wasn't that beautiful! And so was the two-point conversion pass, Montana to Vegas Ferguson. Well now, that's a bit better. That narrowed the score to 34-20 with 7:25 minutes of playing time remaining.

We kicked off to Houston. They didn't get anywhere. By the time we got the ball back, Montana was really ready. He now engineered a 61-yard drive, running and passing. Notre Dame soon scored. There was now only a little over four minutes to play. A short time later we had the ball. Montana completed a pass to the two-yard line and then carried the ball in on the next

Kris Haines

play. This time a two-point pass play to our fleet-footed "good-hands" split end Kris Haines brought the score to 34-28. We had the momentum. But would we get the ball again?

Four minutes left to play. We kicked off to Houston who couldn't get it together. Again, they had to kick to us, with a little more than two minutes left. We got the ball, but again our hopes were dashed when Montana fumbled on a running play after a nice gain of 16 yards. Now it was the Cougar's ball and there was only a little less than two minutes to play. But again, Houston was unable to move the ball. It was their ball, fourth and six. They again had to punt to us.

This could be our opportunity. But no! We were offside on the kick, giving Houston a fourth and one situation! They elected to run for the one yard, in order to hold onto the ball. With complete confidence in their ability to do so, they ran the ball into the line. Notre Dame stopped the play! It was now our ball. We took over—first down—within sight of the goal line. A touchdown would tie the score! Less than a minute left to play. Could we do it? What do you suppose? A time to pray?

Kris Haines scores! The game is tied!

With 28 seconds left, Montana ran the ball for eleven yards. He then threw to his favorite target, Kris Haines, a pass play they practiced all summer. Haines caught the ball. They were eight yards from the goal line, with six seconds to go. Another pass play intended for Haines was incomplete. Two seconds left on the clock. Then the summer's practices paid off.

Montana's pass to Haines in the end zone tied the game as time ran out. Prayers answered—must have been a slow day for Himself to find time for football, but there it was, 34-34. An extra point would win the game, but our regular kicker, Chuck Male, had been injured and was out of the game. The teams lined up again, and our hopes and prayers went up as well. Our second kicker proved dependable. Joe Unis kicked the extra point. What a celebration. He made it! Oh, no! Alas and alack! We were offside. Stay cool and calm, Joe Unis. You just did it. Just do the same

Joe Unis, the kicker and Greg Knafelc, the holder

identical thing again. Five more yards should cause you no sweat on this cold field. Really? Well, don't relax yet!

After the excitement, reality set in. Joe had to kick for the extra point again. Stay loose, Joe, stay cool. Again, the teams lined up. The ball was centered. The holder, Greg Knafelc, hurriedly but accurately set the ball. Joe swung his leg through the kick. Time stopped as the ball shot off his foot—the hush, and then, the cheers! It was good! The ball went straight through between the uprights and above the crossbar. Joe did his job...again...successfully. The final score was 35-34 Notre Dame! Pandemonium broke out among the remnants of the Notre Dame Cotton Bowl attendees, and on the sideline, and on the airwaves. Joe was a hero.

But Joe was not alone—there were others. How many heroes can you have in a game? Joe Unis for sure, kicking the extra point—twice. And we have to include Steve Cichy who ran the blocked kick for a touchdown. And Tony Belden who blocked the kick. Shall we include Joe Gramke and Mike Calhoun who stopped the attempted one-yard plunge by Houston with less than a minute to go? How about the holder, Greg Knafelc, who set the ball just right for Unis? How about the unsung blockers and linemen? And all the others on offense? And the defense? And, oh yes, we should probably mention Joe Montana and Kris Haines. Don't forget them. Joe threw those bullet passes perfectly to Kris Haines who caught the ball. Otherwise, this would not be the "Joe Montana Chicken Soup Story." They do deserve their accolades.

That victory, a "come from behind" win as it was, marked it as one of the great ones in the history of Notre Dame Football. And it certainly cemented Joe Montana in the annals of the "Fighting Irish" for one of the best come-from-behind performances on the list of illustrious Notre Dame football games. Thereby Joe

Montana became one of its most esteemed athletes of all time—
"The Comeback Kid."

AN AFTERTHOUGHT

To say that my daughter and her thoughtful gift of noodle soup
were responsible for the win would be a gross exaggeration.
However, you will have to forgive me if I create that impression
when I relate the total event. It is true that the story has been told
incorrectly in many cases. Some persons make it chicken noodle
soup, being aware of the reputed curative powers of a hot bowl of
chicken noodle soup. Several of my Jewish friends saw to it that
I should have a bowl labeled "Jewish Penicillin" on one side, and
"Chicken Soup" on the other. But no, Mrs. Grass did not make
a chicken noodle soup at that time, nor does she now. She made
a noodle soup, a packet of noodles and mix, which required the
addition of hot water to make a "noodle soup." But there is a
company who uses her noodles in a chicken broth to make "Mrs.
Grass' Chicken Noodle Soup." Nevertheless, for the sake of those
who prefer it that way, let us accept the revisionist version of the
story, with Joe slurping chicken soup. That sounds like the right
thing to do. My Jewish friends concur. I have the soup bowls
labeled "Chicken Soup" on one side and "Jewish Penicillin" on
the other as testimony to that fact. And so that is "the Joe Montana
Chicken Soup Story," one of the better-known legends in the
history of Notre Dame Football.

The "Gipper"

THERE IS NO SHORTAGE of legends at Notre Dame. Among
these, there is one that is always remembered. Stories from an
earlier day abound about George Gipp (the "Gipper")—one of

Notre Dame's legendary football players—who was portrayed by Ronald Reagan in the movie *Knute Rockne, All American*. In that movie, which relates the life story of Notre Dame's beloved football coach, there is a touching scene in which George Gipp, while lying in his hospital bed dying of pneumonia, looks up at Rockne (see photo) and says: "I've got to go, Rock. It's all right. I'm not afraid. Some time, Rock, when the team is up against it and things are wrong and the breaks are beating the boys, ask them to go in there with all they've got, and win just one for the Gipper. I don't know where I'll be then, Rock, but I'll know about it and I'll be happy."

This inspirational story has been told over and again to make the saying "win one for the Gipper" the byword at many a scene. Despite George Gipp's bad behavior as a student, he remains honored and loved as one of Notre Dame's great football players—one of its legends.

Knute Rockne and the "Gipper"

"Rudy"

A MORE MODERN LEGEND is that of "Rudy." His story also occurred during my time with the team. Rudy, Dan Ruettiger, a walk-on, was a determined, strongly built young man, smaller than most of the varsity team players, but tough—a product of the steel mills in Gary, Indiana. He gained a berth on the prep team, working hard, taking a "beating" repeatedly in practice, with nothing to suggest he could one day make the game-day roster. He persevered in his role with the practice teams, never becoming a regular on the varsity, but he was a vital member of the prep team, someone who contributed mightily to the practice sessions preparing the varsity team for its next game.

He earned the love and respect of his fellow players. It was these team members who appealed to Coach Devine to permit Rudy to dress for the last home game of the 1975 season—the final game of his senior year. Coach Devine made a last-minute decision to allow it. Near the end of the game, with Notre Dame ahead, his fellow players further besought the coach to put Rudy into the game. Ultimately, Coach Devine put Rudy in with enough time left for only one more play.

Rudy, a defensive lineman, now had his chance to make history—making all the beatings he had taken in practice with the team even more meaningful—and he made it his big play! On his one play, the last one of the game, Rudy broke through the opponent's line with the snap of the ball from center, eluded one blocker, and brought down the runner from behind. He made the game-ending tackle behind the line of scrimmage bringing the runner down for a loss, the best and only tackle he had ever made in a game. And then it was over! His teammates seized him and hoisted him victoriously on their shoulders to the cheers of his fellow players and the crowd. The story of Rudy remains an inspiration for all. He had entered the hallowed hall of Notre Dame legends.

His story, made into a movie, gave reason for all "walk-ons" to remain hopeful. In the usual routines, the less talented players were relegated to the "prep" squads or dropped from the team. He was one of those "prep" players who became an icon for today's group of aspiring players who live and fight and work diligently at their jobs, in preparing the team for its games. Most of them know there is little likelihood that they will play on game day, but they continue to hope for that break when the coach turns around and calls their number to "Go in for Muldoon," or for whomever. As Gene Paszkiet often said, "Be ready when your number is called." A lesson for all of us!

* * * * *

My personal involvement in this story relates to the fact that Rudy dated Mary Pat, one of my daughters, several times. It didn't last, but it was an interesting development at the time. Rudy, at Notre Dame, is still a legendary figure.

Finale

MANY MORE STORIES could be told of injuries and other conditions, not only in football but in other sports as well—but football produced most of the more serious and frequent injuries with which I dealt. There are many stories that could well be legendary with the proper recognition at the time. Only those qualify which are truly worthy.

As new sports, including women's sports such as soccer, field hockey, crew, lacrosse, and others became varsity sports, the medical team grew in order to take care of the greater number of athletes. Ladies basketball always had its own trainer, but now the same was to be provided for women in other sports. Government fiat, Title IX, required equal facilities for men and women including training rooms, locker rooms, gyms, athletic fields, treatment facilities, etc. As the work increased, my orthopaedic group practice also grew to accommodate these demands. The load was divided and assigned to various members of our group.

South Bend Orthopaedic Associates continues to give their services to Notre Dame and its athletes. There is a pleasure derived from the arrangement, the ability to say, "There goes one of my knees" or "I did his shoulder." The assigned doctors receive tickets for their sport. Surgery is paid for by insurance if and when it becomes necessary. We are fortunate to have good paying practices that allow us to give other services to Notre Dame, pro bono.

We are proud to have earned the confidence of Notre Dame in caring for their clergy, their students, and their athletes.

Dr. Les Bodnar and his wife, Bernardine (Bunny) are honored by "Moose" Krause (Athletic Director Emeritus) and Gene Corrigan (Athletic Director) at halftime ceremonies of the Navy-Notre Dame Game in 1983.

I retired from the Notre Dame scene after 35 years, but I continued my private practice. Later I eliminated the more major surgical procedures and certain other aspects of my work, bringing me a step closer to full retirement. I was then 69 years of age, in good health, and still of sound mind. Over the next eighteen years, I gradually and successively eliminated other aspects of my practice, continuing to the degree of which I felt capable, spending the last five years consulting once a week at a charity clinic, again pro-bono, and the five years before that, assisting my younger associates in surgery. At 87, I fully retired.

I believe I saw medicine in its best years for the actual practice of medicine. During most of those years, the physician occupied a special niche in society. He was honored and privileged. I found myself respected, with grateful patients, the respect of my community, a good living, and all with a marvelous helpmate, my good and loveable wife Bunny, and nine wonderful offspring of whom I am proud—most of whom are now AARPs themselves. Yes, God has been kind. He wasn't too busy. He too was on the job

Dr. Bodnar walking off the field for the last time.

and did it well when He was needed. I am grateful for all He has given me, including those 35 good years with Notre Dame.

As I have written of my personal involvement, and as I note the changes in the game and the practice of medicine, many of which I have witnessed as they came to be, I am reminded that these occurred over the course of a good many years and that I have also added those years to my history. Makes one feel old if he stops to think of it. But that is how it is. "Too soon old" the Dutchman says. How true. Where did it go? And so fast. It also says "Time waiteth not." Even now, it is wasting. And when you know the time is limited, and the supply of it is getting lower, it does cause one to look toward the finale. It may not be too far off. At 98, I probably don't have much farther to go. I hope I did it right.

Afterword

DURING THIS LAST ERA, Coaches Parseghian, Devine, and Holtz were all successful in bringing National Championships to Notre Dame. There were others—good men, good coaches, good teams, and many good players—who followed, but they failed to achieve the degree of success expected at Notre Dame. They tried so very hard, but there are so many variables in the equation that constitute the entire team effort, and if their stars are not all properly aligned at times and success goes astray, the verdict stands that "good" and "better" are not enough at Notre Dame. Only "best" is acceptable. Today, we find that our prayers may have been answered with the advent of Coach Brian Kelly. Many of us were also quite hopeful with the arrival of each of the other coaches, including those who were unsuccessful, so let us wait and see where our new coach will take us. Time will give us the answer. Let us continue to hope that he will be the good news we look for, and right now, it appears that he is. As they say in Irish circles, "Keep the faith."

Supplement

1. Notre Dame players who played professional football after surgical repair of their injuries, 1949-1985

Mark Bavarro	Dislocating Shoulder	N.Y. Giants, 1985-1990, Cleveland, 1992 Philadelphia, 1993-1994
Ted Burgmeier	Knee Meniscus	Kansas City, 1968
Rocky Bleier	Knee Ligaments	Pittsburgh, 1968, 1971-80
George Goeddeke	Knee Ligaments	Denver, 1967-1973
Terry Hanratty	Knee Ligaments	Pittsburgh, 1969-1975 Tampa Bay, 1976
George Kunz	Knee Ligaments	Atlanta, 1969-1974 Baltimore, 1975-1977, 1980
Ray Lemek	Knee Ligaments	Washington, 1957-1961 Pittsburgh, 1962-1965
Alan Page	Dislocating Shoulder	Minnesota, 1967-1978 Chicago Bears, 1978-1981
Walt Patulski	Dislocating Shoulder	Buffalo 1972-1975 St. Louis, 1977
Myron Pottios	Knee Ligaments	Pittsburgh, 1961, 1963-1965 L.A. Rams, 1966-1970 Washington, 1971-1974111
Jeff Weston	Knee Ligaments	1977 (Dr. K. Strong revised 1978) N.Y. Giants, 1979-1982

2. South Bend Orthopaedic Associates:
   Michael Kelbel MD, President

Physician assignments to Notre Dame Athletic Teams:

Football   Brian Ratigan MD, Chris Balint DO,
            David Bankoff MD, Will Yergler MD, emeritus
Hockey   Bob Clemency, MD
Basketball Michael Yergler, MD, Fred Ferlic MD, emeritus
Soccer   Michael Yergler MD
Lacrosse   James Sieradzki MD

Other: Physical Medicine and Rehabilitation:
                Todd Graham MD, Jon Markley MD,
                Angela Stillwagon DO
            Spine Surgeons: Henry DeLeeuw MD,
                Thomas Mango MD
            Hand Surgeons: Randy Ferlic MD,
                A.J. Mencias MD
            General Orthopedic Surgery:
                Henry DeLeeuw MD,
                Henry Kim MD, William Rozzi MD,
                Jeff Yergler MD, Earl Heller, MD.
            Podiatry: Jeffrey Biever DPM,
                Mathew Dinnon DPM.

3. Glossary of Medical Terms

The bones of the joints which have been discussed are labeled in the drawings.

Ligaments are tough fibrous band swhich serve to bind parts of the joint together.

The anterior and posterior cruciate ligaments pass through the interior of the knee.

The medial and lateral collateral ligaments of the knee are located outside the joint.

The capsule is a strong soft-tissue sleeve-like structure enveloping the joint's parts.

The articulating ends of the bones inside the joint are covered with cartilage.

The synovium is the thin smooth membrane lining all other surfaces in the joint.

The meniscus is a fibro-cartilaginous structure spaced between some bones.

Most of the parts of the joint serve to allow stable but limited movement.

The synovium acts to provide lubrication of the joint surfaces

4. Anatomy of the joints

A simplified description of the anatomy of the large joints most frequently injured:

THE KNEE

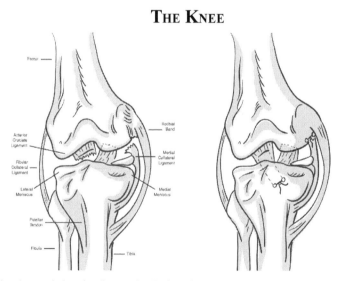

The knee joint is the articulation between the femur, tibia and patella. It is bound mainly by the joint capsule (a sleeve-like structure) and the collateral ligaments on each side of the joint, and by the anterior and posterior cruciate ligaments, which pass obliquely through the interior of the joint. The patella is the "knee-cap" on the front (anterior) of the joint. The bones glide against one another on the smooth surface of cartilage covering the contact areas of the bones. The medial meniscus and lateral meniscus are horse-shoe shaped fibro-cartilaginous structures about the rim of the tiba, separating the femur and the tibia. Muscle action through its tendons adds to the stability of the joint. The fibula along the lateral side of the leg is tethered to the tibia at the knee joint but does not enter the knee joint proper. The medial structures, capsule and ligaments, are usually torn when a valgus (knock-knee) producing force applied to the knee is great enough to tear a cruciate ligament.

THE SHOULDER

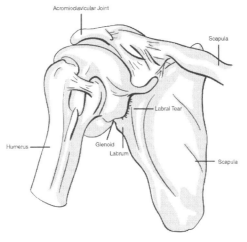

The shoulder joint is the articulation between the shoulder blade (scapula) and the rounded head of the humerus (the bone of the upper arm). The glenoid is the dish-shaped depression in the bony structure of the most lateral part of the scapula forming a shallow socket into which fits the round head of the humerus. The socket is made deeper by a firm fibrous and cartilaginous structure, the glenoid labrum, which encircles the margins of the shallow socket thereby providing a buttress, which with the joint capsule helps, retain the humeral head within the articular structure. Muscle action through its tendons adds to the stability of the joint. The shoulder joint may dislocate when the glenoid labrum is damaged allowing the head of the humerus to migrate out of the confines of the joint.

The clavicle or collar bone and muscles attached to it and the scapula support this shoulder girdle structure against the body. The medial or inner end of the clavicle articulates with the breast bone (sternum) while the outer end of the clavicle joins the scapula by the acromio-clavicular joint. This joint may be separated when the binding ligaments and capsule are stretched and torn, a frequent injury in contact sports.

All of these joint parts are attached by the capsule and various ligaments.

THE ANKLE

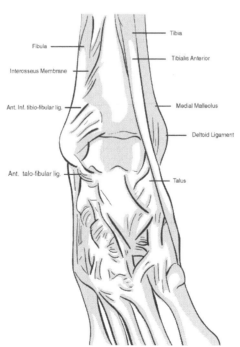

The ankle joint is the articulation between the tibia with its gliding weight-bearing surface and its medial malleolus to stabilize that side of the joint; the fibula with its lateral malleolus stabilizes the join laterally, and the astragalus or talus articulates with the gliding surface of the other bones of the ankle. The capsule, ligaments, and the actions of muscles and their tendons crossing outside the joint add to its stability. The usual ankle sprain is a matter of stretching and tearing of the lateral capsule and ligaments of the ankle.

Surgery

Surgical repair of knee injuries has been modified and improved with the advent of the arthroscope. During the major part of my time at Notre Dame, such surgery was done with wide exposure of the joint to enable the inspection of the joint for adequate evaluation of the injury to the joint and for the performance of whatever corrective measures were to be undertaken. The injuries we have been discussing are primarily to the ligaments, menisci, and articular surfaces.

Menisci may require removal or repair. Articular damage may require smoothing (shaving) or grafting. Ligaments may require repair or replacement. These procedures may be better done through the arthroscope with the further advantage of minimizing blood loss, and allowing more thorough inspection of the joint, and with less risk of post-operative infection than would occur with a joint widely exposed at the time of surgery. It requires a skilled arthroscopist and proper equipment and facilities to gain this advantage of arthroscopic surgery.

During the era when surgical repair of these injured knees was evolving, we found it difficult to access certain parts of the joint despite the wide exposure by which we worked. We soon found that primary repair of the anterior cruciate ligament (ACL) was not likely to succeed with the limited blood supply to this structure, limiting its potential to heal. Replacement of the ACL was necessary. Synthetic materials might do well for limited periods of time before they deteriorated under the mechanical influences on them. Tissues which would survive or become viable were substituted. These procedures taxed the ingenuity and skills of the surgeon. Multiple techniques have been devised and continue to undergo development to restore the stability of the knee joint.

These may involve the use of sections of tissue and bone from the area of the patella, either as a tubular graft still attached

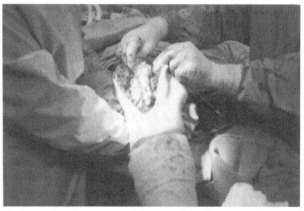

Photograph of interior of knee joint after irrigation and debridement of loose and torn tags of structures.

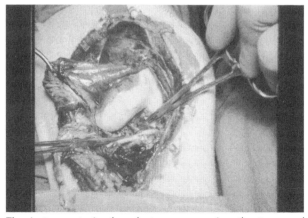

The instruments in the photo are grasping the torn and separated ends of the anterior cruciate ligament.

distally, or as a free graft which would undergo revascularization. Free grafts from the Achilles tendon have also been used. Other methods use structures adjacent to the knee, such as the patellar tendon or one or another of the hamstring tendons or with the use of the fascia lata lateral to the thigh and knee when formed into a tubular structure.

These methods required placement of the insertions of the substitute ACL into the location of its normal attachments to reproduce the mechanical functions for which the ligament was intended. It is virtually impossible to fully re-establish these tissues as nature had arranged them. It is this fact that may result in the varying degrees of residual instability that may occur. The lesser degrees of such dysfunction may be tolerable to the individual with sufficient strengthening of the muscles supporting the knee, although bracing is also necessary at times.

Other structures about the knee, the posterior cruciate ligament, the capsule and collateral ligaments and menisci may require attention at the same surgery. Post-operatively, a variable period of rest and immobilization of the knee follows and later comes the therapy to restore motion and strength before strenuous functional activities are allowed. In spite of the advances in such surgery, some knees are not restored to the degree which enables the functions desired by the patient. And no knee is satisfactorily restored without adequate rehabilitation, a process requiring patient cooperation and work. Although this surgery results in many highly satisfactory results, there are also failures. These latter are grave disappointments in the life of the surgeon, as well as in that of the patient, when dealt to us by the fickle hand of fate.

Acknowledgements

THERE WERE MANY SOURCES contributing to this work, either directly such as an interview with Ara Parseghian, or indirectly as was the advice of Dick Rosenthal who directed me to Missy Conboy for the specific information I needed at the time. Sometime the contribution so derived was lengthy, giving me pages of material for the book, such as the play-by-play descriptions of sequences in the play of some sports events as recorded by Joe Doyle, while at times it was a matter of finding the few words on the internet to complete my description of an episode whose details escaped me.

It would be most difficult to give a weight to each contribution made toward the totality of the events described, therefore I wish to acknowledge all who assisted me in this way, realizing that some few may be missed who should have been included among those to whom I owe thanks. I am sorry to miss anyone and I apologize for that. I will, however, single out just a few who made a greater than usual contribution to the work.

I offer my thanks and appreciation to Ara Parseghian, the late Joe Doyle, Dick Rosenthal, Matt Storin, Joe O'Brien, Missy Conboy, Jim Russ, John Whitmer, Bill and Tom Bodnar, Dr. Randall and Mary Patricia Bay, and the many others to whom I am indebted.

My special thanks to John Heisler and Carol Copley of his media staff for supplying many of the photographs found herein; to my diligent editor Susan Hildebrandt; to the editor and dedicated staff of my publisher, Corby Books; and to Jim Conley and Brian Boulac for their critical reading and commentary in the course of preparation of this manuscript.

I am pleased with the drawings of the anatomic structures in the last few pages of the book, drawn by my granddaughter, Bridget Hildebrandt.

I thank all of them for their help. Thank you.

Leslie M. Bodnar, M.D.

Credits

The images presented are from various sources:

Most are from the archives of Notre Dame and the Media Resource Department at Notre Dame, through the courtesy of John Heisler, Associate Athletic Director for Media Relations, and his assistant, Carol Copley. They are to be found on the following pages: 23, 33, 40, 48, 75, 80, 89, 93, 100, 105, 113, 115, 118, 120, 124, 126, 129, 131, 133, 136, 140, 146, 149, 151, 159, 173, 186, 187, 188, and 191.

Those from the author's personal collection are found on pages 2, 9, 38,76, 82, 105,106, 112, 115, 116, 120,130, 132, 152, 184, 195, and 196.

1. The image of Ara and Katy Parseghian was adapted from a photo captured by "Bubby" Cronin

2 .The photograph of Dr. James Moriarity is from his personal files as is the one from Dennis Gutowski's personal file.

3. The dramatic event captured in the photo of Les Traver's severe injury, showing his leg at a grotesque angle as he is blocked while pursuing an Iowa runner, was taken by an unidentified news-photographer from one of the smaller cities in Central Iowa. I apologize for this lack of identification of the photographer who captured one of those dramatic and devastating actions seen in

football. I also thank the unknown photographer for having sent this to me fifty years ago.

4. The schematic drawings of anatomy were done by my granddaughter, Bridget Hildebrandt.

I thank all of them for their help. Thank you.

Bibliography

THE FOLLOWING SOURCES have been consulted to determine certain facts and figures in order to render a more accurate account of some events detailed in this work. Time and age have dulled my memory of many of these, necessitating my reliance on these records and the written word. Some of these sources have been used to a great extent. If any reader of this history finds any part of it to be inaccurate, I will welcome the correction.

Leslie M. Bodnar, M.D.

Doyle, Joseph. *Fighting Irish.* Charlottesville: Howell Press, 1987.

Walters, John. *Notre Dame Golden Moments.* Nashville: Rutledge Hill Press, 2004.

Dent, Jim. *Resurrection.* New York City: St. Martin's Press, 2009.

Garner, Joe. *Echoes of Notre Dame Football.* Naperville, Illinois: Sourcebooks, Inc., 2001.

Condon, Dave; Grant, Chet; Best, Bob. *Notre Dame Football, the Golden Tradition.* South Bend, Indiana: Icarus Press, 1982.

O'Donoghue, Don H. *Treatment of Injuries to Athletes,* 2nd edition. Philadelphia: W.B. Saunders Co., 1970.

Heisler, John. Senior Associate Athletic Director for Media, Notre Dame.

BCS National Championship Media Guide, 2013.

Notre Dame Football Media Guide, 2004, 2009.

Notre Dame Official Game Day Program, Sept. 11, 2010; Sept. 8, 2012.

Notre Dame Magazine, Summer, 2012.

Glimstedt, O.H. *The Treatment of Athletic Injuries.*
    Publisher and year unknown.
Kelly, Jason. A Technological Knockout for Head Injuries?
    Notre Dame Magazine, Summer 2013, Volume 42,
    Number Two, Page 12.

Index